AF801875

LOOKING PAST THE NEXT PAYCHECK

Table of Contents

Copyright © 2017 by zJet Publishing

All rights reserved. No part of this publication may be reproduced, distributed, or transmitted in any form or by any means, including photocopying, recording, or other electronic or mechanical methods, without the prior written permission of the publisher, except in the case of brief quotations embodied in critical reviews and certain other noncommercial uses permitted by copyright law. For permission requests, write to the publisher, addressed "Attention: Permissions Coordinator," at the address below.

Printed in the United States of America

Second Edition

ISBN: 978-0-9995710-9-5

zJet Publishing

Looking Past The Next Paycheck

Robert L. Robinson

This book is dedicated to the following persons, all of who contributed to making it a reality in their own way:

Eric Bladen, who felt that the book should be written,

Diana C. Titus, the best woman from my wedding, who believed it could be written,

Raymond R. Walker, great friend since May 10 1983, who always looked forward to it being written,

Eric and Nadia Carrillo, my children, who perhaps can find something in the book to better their own lives now that it is written,

And especially to my lovely and supportive wife, Pamela Robinson, who never doubted that someday it would be written.

What Is This Book?

In a nutshell, this book is how to be successful financially. It is based on how I overcame obstacles to succeed. These are the techniques that I used to turn around my financial life. I was broke, I was drunk, I was so far in debt that at one time the credit card company sent me a letter that if I tried to use their card again, the merchant was under direct orders to con- fiscate the card. Today I have no credit card debt, a number of income properties, a new house, good credit, and am self employed and comfortable. My wife and I take a cruise every couple of years. We just returned from Hawaii. The one before was about 18 months prior to the Panama Canal. This book tells you how I did it. How I got out of debt. How I established good credit (not that tough—paid my bills and skipped the easy way out routine). How I learned to control my money. How I took charge of my financial life. This book is a "how-to" manual with true-life occurrences tossed in. In a nutshell, this is the system that worked for me. The hands-on methods, the philosophy, the growing understanding of finance.

Who Is This Book For?

Are you living paycheck to paycheck? Debt up to your eyeballs? Do you consider a car payment, credit card payments, and rent as a normal part of life that will always be with you? Do you consider equity in your car an indication that you need to either refinance or buy a new car? And most important, do you want more out of life than the same old grind year in and year out? If so, then this book is for you. If. If you are willing to make a commitment. If you are willing to change old habits and learn new ones, and if you are willing to wrap your mind around the fact that it is possible for you to be successful. You have to believe. You have to believe because you have to have an all-consuming desire, and you can't have an all-consuming desire if part of your energy is being used to spark that voice in the back of your head voicing nagging doubts. So how do you believe? You learn to recognize reality, and you break your all-consuming desire into a concrete, mathematically proven, reality based, outcome observable master plan.

But Is This Book For You?

I've stated who this book is for, but you must determine if it is for you. Are you tired of a dead end job, or is the monotony what you are happy with? Do you want more out of life, or are you content to watch others advance while you go through the daily grind? Are you secure living from paycheck to paycheck, or would you rather have control over you life? If you are someone that is looking for a better life only if there is no effort involved, and you truly believe that working forty hours a week five days a week when you are told to, doing what you are told, and limiting your ambitions to sleeping late on Saturday after a Thank God Its Friday is what life is all about, then this book is not for you. If you are content in blissful ignorance, you have already risen to your level of existence. But for the rest of us, there is this book.

PART I

The Philosophies

Get Your Head Straight And Make A Commitment To Succeed

This book is a hands-on guide to getting on the road to financial freedom. It is written for Joe and Jill Average. If you already have more money than you know what to do with and are looking for hot stock tips or the commodity of the month, you bought the wrong book. Sorry, no refund. By the same token, if you are just dumb as dirt, a habitual joiner looking for another get rich quick scheme to blow next week's paycheck or the kid's college fund on, you too bought the wrong book. Again, no refund. Now, back to what this book is. As I said, it is for Joe and Jill Average. Not as Joe and Jill are portrayed on the TV sitcoms, but real life Averages. Don't you love those TV sitcom "averages"? They work minimal hours at an entry level job, and have enough money for everything that their hearts desire. Art may imitate life, but that ends with sitcoms. Whatever that form of art is imitating, it's not life. Real life "averages" never seem to get ahead. We work hard, do our job, manage to keep half a step ahead of the bill collector (on a good week), see no way we will ever retire, heck, even affording more of a vacation than a week at home on the couch watching the soaps is way out of reach. I say "we" because I used to be in the same boat with you. I got ahead of the dead end game, and I will show you how you can, too. And, like I said at the beginning, this is a hands-on book. I am going to take you by the hand and show you how to start to get things in order and pull ahead of the pack. And we will start today! This is not a book of Rah! Rah! Nor is it a book of theories that "should" work. We are not even going to talk about statistical anomalies like they are do-able plans. Instead, I am going to take you by the literary hand (hands on, remember?) and walk you through what to do to take charge of your financial life, step by step, and how to bring the truth to the light of day. Be prepared, the truth may be that on your current course, you can never be financially comfortable. If this is the case, you are going to have a tough choice to make—better yourself and your situation for a chance at success (which will require sacrifice and work), or stay the course for certain failure. But you will know, and knowledge is power. And with that knowledge, you can right your course and sail on to a better place.

The Very First Rule

Before we even start, there is a rule that you should understand. You don't have to accept it, but if you don't, it won't be any less true. Opportunity and need are not friends. They seldom hang around together. When you have a real financial need, opportunity is usually somewhere unreachable. And when opportunity is doing handstands in front of you, need is not rearing its head. Get it understood, when you have the opportunity to make money or better yourself, do it. Don't blow it off with the excuse that other things are more important, unless you know for a fact that when need does return, those other things are going to carry you through.

About Theories

Theories are nice, and at the peak level of any endeavor, there are going to be contradicting theories about what is best. From the various offenses in football to the different disciplines in the martial arts, to the various strategies and vehicles for investing, there will always be differences of opinions. What works today may not be the best in a different situation tomorrow. But this is at the top level. When you are dealing with the basics, there is a lot less ambiguity, and a lot more concrete rules. Good news! That is the level that we will be beginning with—discussing income and expenses, not the merits of mutual funds versus income properties. Keep in mind, at the level that we are at, we are not even ready to partake in any of these theories, let alone to discover which theory is best. We are looking to build the basic foundation that will allow us to step up and decide what theory is right for us at that specific time. If we don't master the basics, no theory will matter, because we won't have the resources to effectively undertake the task.

Hurdles, Obstacles, And Excuses

As you pursue financial success there will be hurdles and obstacles thrown in your way. There will be people in your life that complicate your achieving your goals. You have to recognize these people and handle them accordingly. Ignoring them will not make the problem go away. The same holds true with problems that you yourself are the cause of. They too must be dealt with.

Then there is the excuse. The excuse is simply why you or someone else tells you that you can't succeed. Your age and your education level are two of the biggest excuses. One you can do nothing about but get older, and the other you can do something about, and much easier than many would have you believe.

Being Milked By Others

If you have a dependent, be it a parent, a sibling, or a spouse that you are supporting, you really must analyze the situation and see if this someone is on your side to help you succeed, or if they really don't care about your goals and ambitions and are just using you for a free ride. Quite often, the dependant—be they significant other, parent, sibling, whatever—will prove to be very supportive, take the task at hand very seriously, and really motivate and encourage you to do the very best possible, possibly even much better than you could have achieved on your own. However, they could also turn out to be the dreaded Free Rider! The Free Rider is the master of the guilt manipulation, and you must overcome this or you are pretty much guaranteeing your own failure. The master-mooch will never let up, never take responsibility, and will be content to have absolutely nothing tomorrow as long as his immediate desires are met today. Besides, worrying about tomorrow is your job, that's what he keeps you around for. The only way I have ever found that is effective in dealing with this manipulator is with the strong-arm tactic. Your way or get out. If the person is supposed to pay towards room and board, don't wait until the bill is due; collect the money now in advance, or put him out until he has it. Don't be faced with counting on the money at the end of the month and getting nothing but the sad story. If the leech doesn't pay anything, but runs the bills through the roof, put a limit on things: Phone bill goes over so much money, they pay the difference or no phone (or get out). I tell you from experience, lots of it, that firm and consistent is the only long term solution. It may sound harsh, but once you put it into focus, it really isn't. You can let the bum run you into ruin, or you can be strict and succeed and actually be able to support the freeloader in the years to come. And when your resolve begins to fade, just ask yourself how much you will love each other when you are living on the corner of the freeway in your new refrigerator box. My bet is that it will be you in the refrigerator box while your poor incapable loved one moves on to another supportive sucker.

Monkey On Your Back

An unsupportive person dragging you down is bad enough, but doing it to yourself is something that you have to face and conquer before you can hope to make permanent advancements. Addiction is addiction, it doesn't matter if it is alcohol, drugs, tobacco, lottery tickets, trips to the casino, fast food, excessive collecting, whatever. Making it to the front of the pack is going to take undivided attention, and there is no room for the monkey on your back. If you can't just kick the monkey to the curb, give him a rain check; he may just go away. Almost twenty years ago I was deeply in love with beer. It wasn't a need as much as a grand desire. A six pack in the first twenty minutes that I was home, and three more six packs (at least) before hitting the sack (or couch, or, as was often the case, the floor). This was how I spent a large chunk of the decade of the eighties. No, I wasn't addicted, I could quit anytime that I wanted to. I just didn't want to quit, that was all. But deep down, I wanted to succeed. And, no surprise, I wasn't succeeding. So I made a deal with myself. I would apply myself to making my first million, and then I would return to my true love, the golden nectar of the gods. The following morning I arose and set out to make a fortune for my beer and I. Cold turkey. I never "quit". But I have never had another drink, and I have come to the realization that my passion and I may be parted for life; I may never return to my one time love. The love affair is over. So take from the story what you will, but forget about illness and lack of control and everything else that is an excuse for failure. If you want to succeed, you can. If you want an excuse for failure, don't look at the monkey on your back, look in the mirror.

Money Is Bad

Every so often I will run into someone that actually has been brainwashed into believing that money is bad. If you are one of these mislead souls, you cannot succeed until you wipe this silly notion out of your head. A bit of common sense mixed with a spoonful of reality is all that is required to see that the "money is bad" notion is a crock designed to separate the gullible from either their money or their labors without just compensation. No one has ever looked at a hungry child or someone in need of medical help and felt that this is a good thing, since the money required for food and medicine is evil. Only a moron would argue that you can do more good without money than with money. The worship of money may well be bad, but the pursuit of money to provide for yourself and loved ones, as well as any that you wish to contribute to, is not. Fact of reality: The wealthy do more to help the needy and to improve life for all of mankind than the poor. The poor do not create jobs, do not fund medical research, and do not create opportunities. The wealthy do. And often, the only difference between the wealthy and the poor is a desire to put forth the extra effort to succeed.

Don't Get Greedy

A natural offshoot of being told that money is bad is the "don't get greedy" beat down. It's okay if you make enough money to cover (barely) your day-to-day bills, but if you do anything beyond this, you are greedy. This one is often paradoxical: If you don't go the extra distance for free, you are lazy, but if you do go the extra distance and make a profit from it, you are greedy. This concept comes from one of three places: Either someone that has heard it so much that they are conditioned into believing it, someone who doesn't want to go the extra distance or put out the effort to really succeed and certainly doesn't want anybody around that does, or somebody that wants to separate you from your money and labors without compensation, but doesn't want to support you or lose your philanthropy.

Age

Let' talk about age a bit. Oh my God, I never thought that there were so many things in life that a person could be too old for when they are not. One of the easiest ways to cop out is to play the age card. Also, one of the easiest ways for someone to bail on helping you is to play your age card. Let me explain a bit.

I had an Uncle that did some work with NASA. About the end of my sophomore year of high school, he passed on some space stuff that caught my attention. I decided that I now knew what I wanted to do with my life. I wanted to work for NASA. Somehow it came about that the best way to do that was to get a degree in physics in college. OK, no problem. I went to the high school counselor full of high hopes the following Monday morning and let it be known that I wanted to pursue a physics degree in college and that I was ready to start preparing for that goal. Nope, sorry, too late. If that is what I wanted to do I should have taken the appropriate classes my freshman year of high school. That ship has sailed. I know now that that was not true, but back then I figured that the guy whose full time job was to guide me knew what he was talking about. Twice more I would be burned by this type of expert, once more actually by this very same one. I will relate those incidents to you a bit later. Right now let's stay on topic of age.

Having missed the physics-in-college boat, I enlisted in the army at the ripe old age of nineteen. I served four years as a missile radar repairman. At the end of my term, I exited the army to apply my new found skill set in the civilian world.

Heading straight to the unemployment office, I quickly found that much of the civilian population either did not have an air defense missile system in their back yard, or if they did, they had no openings for someone to keep its radars operational. But that was all right. The working for my uncle Sam had taught me that I had to be flexible. I sat with the counselor at the unemployment office and we went through the listings of jobs that I was qualified for. Most of them were the same jobs that I had been qualified for four years prior before I got all that good military training. It seems that there are always openings in my life for selling shoes for minimum wage. As the counselor flipped the pages, she skipped right over one that looked like something with a future. "Hey, what's that?" Silly me, how naïve I must be even to inquire! I was promptly told that that was a union job. I had no clue what that meant, and said as much. I was informed that for a union job, you have to start out as an apprentice, and at the rickety old age of twenty-three, I was much too old for that. Dang, way laid by the old age thing again!

Are you seeing the pattern here? Two lessons can be extracted from the above incidents. First, when the "expert" doesn't tell you what you want to hear, find another expert. Second, the age thing is often nothing but a way for someone to keep from helping you without outwardly refusing to do their job. Age is also often used simply to filter out the applicants. If someone tells you that you are too old for something and you accept that, instantly there is one less person to be dealt with.

Something else that often comes up related to age is when someone looks at doing something that requires more than a little time—getting out of debt, getting an education, things of this nature—they always figure what their age will be when the goal is achieved, as if that has any bearing on the goal. For instance, someone at thirty looking at something that will take five years to achieve will often speak out "I don't know, if I do that I will be thirty-five by the time I'm finished". News flash, in five years you will be five years older if you try to achieve a goal or not. If you are still on this earth sucking in air in five years time, you will be five years older than you are now. Period. You may be out of debt, or you may be even further buried in obligation. You may have the coveted degree, or you may still be as uneducated as you were five years prior, but you will still be five years older.

Keep this in mind. You will never again be younger than you are today. So when someone plays the age card on you, think about it a second and ask yourself if you are really ready to give up that easily. This is how old you are. Also, keep in mind that when you are looking to the future, a future age is much older than it will be when you have passed it. Huh? Thirty-five when you are twenty-five is much older than thirty-five is when you are forty-five.

Education

This talk of age has overlapped a bit into the topic of education. Education is a tool, and it can be a key. It is not a miracle cure. It does not by itself make someone a better person. It can help you with your future and it is obtainable, if you want it.

Many times, education is used as a filter for a job. For example, the position may call for a two-year degree to apply. No two-year degree, no application. Cuts out lots of applicants. It does not mean that you need the education to do the job, it simply means that you need the education to apply for the job. Big distinction. This is important because many people, particularly those who have never attended college, are of the impression that how to do the job is actually taught in college, and without the college you cannot do the job. In some instances, this might be true. Doctors come to mind. But in many cases, it is not true. I can honestly say that I learned a lot in college. It has enhanced my appreciation of certain things, and sharpened my critical thinking in some areas. However, very, very little of what I learned in college has played any kind of bearing in my professional life. Remember a few lines up where I mentioned that the job might require a two-year degree? Much of the time, it doesn't even matter what the degree is in. Just that you have a degree. It filters out the applicants, as I stated earlier, and in some people's eyes, it identifies you as not being a quitter. You have to wade through a lot of nonsense and put up with a lot of over-educated morons to get a degree. If you got the degree, maybe you won't walk out on the job the first time it gets really ignorant in the work place. Of course, there is a flip side to this theory as well. There are career students in the world that while highly educated, are not suited for any kind of employment. I know, I have had the misfortune of working with a few of them. How they actually got to work by themselves every day was a grand mystery.

Now, whereas a college degree may get your foot in the door, it does not automatically make you a better person, or for that matter, even better suited for the job. This is a fact that is lost on many college graduates. Because someone has not been educated in the hallowed halls does not necessarily make him stupid. Some of the most intelligent people that I have ever met have never stepped inside a college. And, in fact, many of them hold a college education in a sort of awe that should be reserved for saints and other metaphysical beings.

I mentioned earlier that I joined the army at the age of nineteen. In basic training, there was a fellow that was entirely too good to be there. He was a tall, skinny fellow who had a five-year degree in communications. I was totally in awe of the man, and never dared speak a word to such a misplaced dignitary. He, to his own great misfortune, felt that I was right. He went through weeks of a hell of his own design. He was an enlisted man, as memory serves me, a Private First Class, the same rank as I. He had earned his rank via his college, and I had earned mine by attending high school JROTC.

As I stated, I was in awe of this man, and this man was in awe of himself. The college man refused to participate in the daily chores required of new soldiers. He was too educated to scrub toilets, and definitely would not scrub toilets while there were plenty of the uneducated masses to do it. He would lower himself to supervising such a task, if really necessary, but even this would be a grand waste of his superior intellect.

Sorry to say, the drill sergeants did not place this individual on the same pedestal that I did. He was sent to a military readjustment unit, and then if memory serves me, was discharged from the army. Fired, if you will. Regrettably for this man, you have to go through a lot of misery before your termination of employment when you work for Uncle Sam's military.

As I have alluded to earlier, I did finally attend college. I had some continuing education classes in real estate prior to joining the army, and then pursued a college education after serving in the army twice. I was about thirty-one years old when I returned to college. It took a lot of knocks up side the head before I realized that I needed to get there.

Now, you might be wondering that if I am all so smart as to write a book on how to do things why it took me so many years just to get to college. Well, this book is not because I am all so smart, but rather because I am so stupid that I have made most every mistake known to man, and still persevered to the point of quasi-success.

Back to the question of why it took so long for me to go to college. Remember the story a bit earlier about when I wanted to go to college and major in physics? Well, a couple of years later I would once again receive outstanding help and support from this same counselor. Approaching graduation from high school, I had been told by my mother that there was no money to send me to college, so don't expect it. OK, fine. I was called to the counselor's office where he would counsel me on all of the options available to me if I chose to pursue a college path. And as I would learn years later, there is money available —lots of money. In America, not having the money is not an excuse for not going to college. There are grants and there are loans. The less you have, the more is available. And the great thing about grants is you don't have to pay them back! If that isn't great enough, there are plenty of companies out there that are more than willing to send you to college, or at least cut a check to help with the bills, if you will just write a paper telling them why they should do so.

I knew none of this. I knew that I had no money and my mom said she and my dad were not paying to send me to college. So I showed up for my counseling appointment knowing nothing. This would not change. My counseling went something like this:

"Mr. Robinson, what do you plan on doing after you graduate from high school?"

"Get a job, I guess. I don't have any money."

"Alright, Mr. Robinson, if you will sign here saying that we had this little meeting, I won't take up any more of your time."

Yea, this clown led the charge on the declining quality of our modern education system.

If you have decided to go to college, keep a few things in mind. Higher education is a business. A business about making money. Not for you, for the school. Fact of life. You may not like it, but it is the truth. Yes, you may find professors that have your best interest at heart, and you will find some that could not care less if you succeed or not. You will even find those entrepreneurial ones that see you as a way to line their own pockets with cash. How clandestinely they do it will be the interesting part.

Before we launch into lessons learned from the realm of higher learning, it might be of note how someone as stupid as me figured he should go to college. Sometimes I have to be hit over the head with a two by four a number of times before realization dawns.

I interviewed for a number of jobs after leaving the military the first and second time (Yes, after getting out the first time, eighteen months later I was back in camouflage.) Everywhere I went, including a number of defense contractors, the story was the same. They would ask how much education I had, and I would list out all of my military training. They would reply that they did not consider the military schools as education. Then they would ask how much experience I had, I would tell them about my years in the army, and they would tell me that they did not consider the military as experience. Further, they would explain to me that with no education and no experience, there was not much they could do for me.

I returned to selling cars, which I had done when I first graduated from high school (failing miserably to make money in any quantity), and again when I exited the army the first time (actually making a living wage one month). I proved to myself that somehow in the four years since my last failure that I had not gained any useful insight into profiting from the lucrative auto sales industry. That is to say, I almost starved.

Exiting the auto business, I landed a job as a warehouse manager for a carpet company. This lasted about six months. I was given a promotion to the big six dollars an hour (while supporting a wife, two kids, and five in-laws) and given the lecture to get used to it, it would be the last raise I would ever see with that company until the day I retired. Minimum wage was about five dollars and fifteen cents an hour at that time. Somehow, the light bulb finally illuminated and I realized I needed an education.

Before we go too much further, keep in mind that the same jobs that would not even talk to me before I went to college would pay much larger bucks years later both in salary and in consulting after I had the college, even though the knowledge they were paying for I already possessed before ever stepping into a college classroom.

When I finally decided that college was where I needed to be, I spent a Saturday taking placement tests. After the placement tests, I took my results to a counselor.

Remember I mentioned that many of the profiteers are only different in how clandestinely they lined their pockets? Here is an example of the old "what's good for the college is good for me" pirate. Looking at my scores, the counselor informed me that I would need to take a class in college reading. Mandatory non-college-credit remedial course to improve my reading score. I had no problem believing it. I had never been to college, of course I was not at college level! Let me count out the money...

On the first day of class, the teacher explained how we had taken a test in the placement testing that had indicated that we should be here in the class. At the end of the class we would take the test again to show our improvement in reading skills. This teacher was one of those who actually was there for the students and not to seek additional riches. A wonderful lady, one of many college teachers and professors that I would meet in the coming years who cared about the well being of their students. Among the self-centered scum who cared about nobody's well being other than their own. She talked to each student one by one, reviewing their test scores, and letting them know what they could expect from the class. When she got to me, she looked at my paperwork and asked why I was there. I told her because of my reading score. She said she didn't understand. Now I didn't understand and asked her to explain. Well, for the test that they administer, which would be the same test at the end of the semester, I had already scored a maximum score, so no improvement on the test was possible. See that? I was getting educated to the way things really are already!

Not all of the scoundrels were as stealthy as the counselor that had sold me the unneeded class. I'm sure that he could have pleaded that he felt that the class would still benefit me, or perhaps he could tell how he was just following orders. Others of his ilk would be much more transparent in their duplicity. Two of my favorite examples were actually instructors of a friend of mine. But as illustrations, I cannot think of two more deserving con men.

The first of the two was a math instructor. Now, I have no way of knowing who in the math department was making the mint off of this little scam, but I do know that the instructor did not raise any question about the ethics involved. As I said, my friend was taking a math course. Not some new, just discovered math, if there is such a thing, but something like Intro to Calculus. The knowledge has been around forever. Think about it, when was the last new thing discovered that would be included in an introduction to calculus course? Onward with the story. My friend paid for the course, bought the book (not a small amount of money for that book, either) and then eight weeks into the sixteen week course, was required to buy another just published book on the same subject that the class would now be using. For one hundred bucks. Same subject matter in both books. Math. Is the scam apparent, or what?

But wait, it gets better. Same friend, another class. The instructor of the class had written a book, but apparently couldn't get it published. Or maybe there was more profit in his pocket the way he did it—no pesky publishing company to cut into the profits. Regardless of the cause, this was the book that was to be used in class. Purchase mandatory. Every Friday everyone in the class had to go down to a little copy center a few blocks from the college and buy copy machine copies of the next chapter of the book. Loose papers. For thirty five bucks! Every week! For most of sixteen weeks! License to steal, or what?

And because it calls itself a college class does not guarantee the quality of education, either. For instance, I took a class in BASIC, the computer language. Using the word "class" is a true stretch. The teacher would come in and tell us to type in a program from the book. No instruction, just type it in. Her theory was that the typing in of the program would enhance our typing skills, and when it did not work because of a mistyped character, we would have to find the mistyping and that this would enhance our debugging skills. When it did work, we would see what we had typed and this would teach the computer language. Luckily, I already knew how to program in BASIC. Oh, yea, just to enhance your under standing that it is all about the money, computer classes were required for my degree plan of computer programming and could not be tested out of.

That's right. You had to pay for the class even if it was not going to teach anything and even if you had the knowledge to pass the final exam before you even stepped into the class.

One more tale of woe before I stop beating on the poor old higher education racket. When I started college, there was some kind of test that everyone enrolled in the college had to take. State law. If you did not pass it by a certain time in your college career, you would be restricted to only taking non-college credit remedial classes. So, needless to say, it was imperative that that I take this test. And what a pony show it was. Many times I was told that I had to take it, that they had got me scheduled for a Saturday morning on the other side of town, how it would take all morning, get a good night's sleep, how my entire future hinged on this test, and on and on. Oh, yea, also how I had to pay thirty-five dollars, can we have the money now?

So I paid, I tested, congratulations—I passed, and then I was told that of course, since I was prior service military, I was exempt, but since I had chosen to take the test anyway, of course there was no refund. These incidental horror stories are not in any way meant to imply that college is bad, that an education is bad, or that the pursuit of education is bad, or even that it is not a worthy endeavor. College is fine for what it is. It will get you into applying for positions that were closed to you before. It will introduce you to new ways of thinking that you have never previously been exposed to. It will present you with core courses that you will spend the rest of your days wondering why you were required to attend them. Who knows, if you apply what you are taught and embrace the education, you may even come out a better person than you went in as, but it will be you who causes this change, not the college. Above all else, education is a tool. An often-necessary tool, a great tool to have in your possession, but only a tool. It is something that will help you progress in life. Getting the education is the barely the beginning, not the end. Keep in mind as well that while college can improve your financial well being, the people of the college are often there primarily for there own financial well being.

What About Money For College

There is money out there from just about every source imaginable for college. Even better, much of it is a gift. Not a loan. Loans are also available, but should be considered as a last resort. When everybody from your Uncle Sam to the people that make the food that you eat for dinner and everyone in between are looking for worthy people to receive the gift of their money for the pursuit of education, why accept money that you have to pay back?

The first thing that you have to do is find where these grants are at. You do this through the financial aid department of whatever college you are trying to attend. The good news is that the college is the end recipient of the money you are trying to acquire, the bad news is that their employees don't always concern themselves with what is in their employers best interest. The fact that it is best for them to find the money to put you into school doesn't always trickle down to the individual that you are looking to for help. Too often, this person sees no correlation at all between their collecting a paycheck and actually doing the job that they are being paid to do. You might have to contact more than one person in the school's financial aid department, you will need to be persistent, and once somebody decides to open the hidden tome of financial aid opportunities, you will need to wade through it to find grants that are applicable to you. There are grants for pretty much every occupation as well as every demographic that you might be a member of. One bright spot about the pain in actually finding these grant opportunities is that it eliminates a huge amount of your competition—the other free money seekers. There is an amazing thing about people searching for free money—many of them are not willing to do much to procure it.

Once you locate the grants that you qualify for, start applying. There is usually an essay involved, so start cranking out essays. And don't stop. Don't expect to receive every grant that you apply for. Don't even expect to receive every other one. I was extremely lucky. Of the three non-government grants that I applied for, I received one. Which I won by default. No one else applied! Not that this made the group awarding the check very happy. Originally, the winner was to be awarded the money at a dinner ceremony. Well, the end of the award competition came and went, and they only had one entry—mine. The organization awarding the grant was in a bind. They were bound to deliver the scholarship, but I was not the ideal candidate they had in mind. Instead of being a young lad with stars in his eyes, I was a relatively older, crusty ex-sergeant fresh from defending the constitution of the United States from all threats, foreign and domestic. Not really a welcome stereotype to this group. There was himming and hawing, the dinner and award ceremony was delayed, and delayed and finally cancelled with the check being sent directly to the college's financial aid department. I never even got a chance to meet or thank anyone associated with the money. You know what? It spent just as well as if I had met them and they did like me!

In addition to the money, I took away a very important lesson from this experience. Had this opportunity been posted on a board somewhere where anyone wanting to apply could easily find the information, there is no doubt in my mind that I would not have won the money. In fact, judging by the way that the events played out, I truly believe that had anyone else in the world applied, I would not have won. Tough. I did win, and I did receive the money!

Master Price Guide

Some people seem to believe that there is a master rule book about how much something is worth, how much they should be paid, the value of a degree, etc. Right up front, nothing is worth anything but what someone will pay for it. Period. It is not even worth what someone did pay. Maybe a particular marble sold for ten thousand dollars. Look at the facts, and you might find that there was one guy with more money than common sense who had a dream about buying a marble, so he did. He now has the marble, he is not looking to buy another one. Nobody else particularly wants the marble. The fact that the buyer paid ten thousand dollars for the marble does not make it and all the other marbles in the world worth ten thousand dollars. If there is no one else in the world willing to pay anything for the marble, it is essentially a worthless marble that sold for ten thousand dollars. More a testament to one man's foolishness than setting an incredible value on a marble.

When a price guide on a particular item is published it may be a number of things. It may reflect what buyers have paid in the past. It may be an offer to sale and be a price for which the item can be bought. It is not a declaration of value. The only thing that can set a value is a willing buyer and a willing seller agreeing on a price. And even then the value is only legitimate if there are other buyers and other sellers willing to honor that price.

And so it is when you read about the dollar value of a college education. Pure statistical non-sense. The unemployment lines are full of highly educated persons, as the ranks of the super wealthy are bulging with individuals that never finished college (some never began). Education is what you do with it. The person makes the use of the education, not the other way around!

Life Lesson On Not Screwing Up A Good Thing

If there was one thing that the army harped on, it was to be flexible. And as hard as this is to accomplish, it is the truth. You have to be flexible in everything you do, when it is for your benefit. This does not mean to go through life willy-nilly, but rather learn to analyze the situation and determine with an open mind if the business as usual approach is the way to handle it, or if it is more advantageous to you to be flexible in your course of action. Once again, this can be exemplified in a real life story.

In the army, we had a coffee pot in our work area. The coffee grounds came from the mess hall. No cost. Great deal. One day, a fellow who had been with the unit before rejoined the unit. The first thing to pop into his little head while enjoying a free cup of coffee was that we needed a coffee fund. The conversation went something like this:

> *"We should have a coffee fund and charge by the cup."*
>
> *"Why?"*
>
> *"So we can pay for the coffee!"*
>
> *"But it's free. We get it from the mess hall."*
>
> *"It doesn't matter. We should have a coffee fund. That's how everybody does it."*

Now, a person of even a small bit of common sense would realize that when you get something for free, you don't need money to pay for it. However, the army is run by rank, not common sense, so within a very short time, there was a sign by the coffee pot with the price of a cup of coffee written on it, and an empty can to catch the money. Before the can had caught enough money to pay for the ink on the sign, let alone any coffee, our contact from the mess hall came in, saw the sign, saw the money can, and cut us off. In a nutshell, no more free coffee because "everybody did it like that".

In The Beginning ...

To know where we are going, we have to know where we are. Very basic. Where we are at is simply what we have, what we owe, where the money is coming from and how much, and where is it going and how much. From there, we can expand it out to how reliable is the incoming money, and how necessary is the outgoing expense.

First, let's discuss a term and a concept and learn how this concept is very important to our financial well being. The term is fungible. Money is fungible. What does that mean? Let's learn through a little project.

Project 1

Take an empty glass. Fill it 1/4th full of water. Now fill it the remainder of the way full. Now remove the original 1/4th. Ahh, not so fast. I said remove the original 1/4th not just 1/4th. Can't do it can you? That is how money is—fungible. If you find twenty dollars on the ground, and you then work until you are ready to drop for another twenty dollars, you have forty dollars. Period. Forty dollars. Not two types of twenty dollars; there is only one type. You have to understand this concept. You have to respect the money. The twenty dollars that you found on the ground has no less value than the twenty dollars that you worked so hard for simply because you found it. It all spends the same. To view money any other way is either you deceiving yourself, or someone else deceiving you.

Often you will see government being deceptive in this manner. They will make a large expenditure and then explain that it didn't cost the taxpayer anything because it came from some other form of money, i.e., it's federal money, it's confiscated money, it's grant money, etc. The question is seldom asked why this money wasn't used for something the taxpayers are having to pay for. "Oh, don't feel bad, we couldn't use that twenty dollars to pay part of the forty dollars that you owe—it was found money. You know all tax money has to come from your front pocket to be used for those kinds of expenses." Sounds like a rip off line that it would take a moron to fall for, doesn't it? Well, believe it or not, the government does it to us every day, and even more disturbing, many of us do it to ourselves at every opportunity! The government does it to us, and we do it to ourselves because we don't know where our money comes from, what it can and should be doing while have it, or where it goes when it leaves.

What Is Economics?

It helps to have an understanding of economics at the very basic level and be able to apply it to our own personal situation.

You cannot do everything you need yourself. You cannot build your house while at the same time hunt for your food and prepare it and defend the house while you eat the food. Because of these shared needs, people work together to make a civilization work. You work to build my roof and I work to feed you three chickens. There you go, that simple barter is the foundation of economics. I trade you the fruit of my labor for the fruit of yours. But what if I need my roof right now because it is raining, but you just had lunch and don't need your chicken meal right now? Easy, I give you a piece of paper representing the meal. When you get hungry, bring me the piece of paper, and I will feed you your three chickens. With the piece of paper standing in for the actual item, we have invented money.

You might notice that this entire transaction is between two people. This is very important, and not as obvious as you might think. Constantly I am confronted with people that think they can work without dealing with people. Money only has a value if there is someone else willing to accept it. Often the same people that think they can have an economy without dealing with people are the ones that look down their noses at salesmen. Guess what? Economy is based on sales, the exchange or barter of one thing for another. Everyone that is not involved in the face-to-face selling is in a support facility that is dependent upon the salesman for his daily pay. Think about it. How necessary is an accounting clerk if there is no money coming in or going out? About as necessary as a computer programmer writing programs with nobody to use them. The exchange of goods and services is what it is all about.

And, to round it out, there are only three occurrences that effect your financial well being: How much you spend, how much you make, and how much your investments make. How much you spend is simply the money going out. Voluntary, involuntary, expected, surprise, none of these things matter. Money going out is money going out.

But there are two kinds of money coming in: Money you make and money that your investments make. One is dependant upon your labors, physical, mental, or both. And one, ideally, is not. This is what differentiates the two. If you are the founder a business that you run and you take a few days off, the money might still come in. This is not your investment working for you, this is you coasting on your work. If you invest a chunk of money in a blue chip stock and then go on cruise around the world, presumably the stock will do the same for you that it would have if you had never gone. Try that test with your own company. One day, without telling anyone, go on a cruise around the world. Want to gamble on if you will even have a company when you return?

We Need A Master Plan That Defines Where We Are And Where We Are Going

It is a cliché, it might be over stated at times, but it is true. It is very hard to plan where we are going if we do not know where that might be. Think about it a second. If I send you out in the morning to pursue your fortune and I tell you that you need to return with enough money for a room and food tonight or else you won't eat and you will sleep outdoors on the ground in the rain, it would definitely help you to know how much you need to earn today to afford that meal and that room. Knowing how much money we need to make today is a short-term version of knowing where we are going.

What is the Master Plan

Even though the "Master Plan" may sound like something metaphysical or perhaps designed to either connect you with the next plane of existence or at the very least save your mortal soul from eternal damnation, it is nothing of the sort. It is awareness. Plain and simple. Awareness of what you want out of life. Awareness of what is required for day-to-day living. Awareness of how to achieve these things. Awareness of where your resources are coming from and where they are going to. In a nutshell, how are you going to get what you want out of life? That is the one sentence description of a master plan.

The Mantra Is Holistic, Consistent, and Persistent With Tenacity

Money is fungible, and because of this we need to maintain a holistic view of our finances. We need a certain amount for our day-to-day expenses, we need a certain amount to get out of debt, and we need a certain amount to achieve our master financial goal. Each of these amounts are amounts of money. Not amounts of earned money, or found money, recycling money or babysitting money, forgotten money, or even birthday gift money. There are no such things. There is only money. To determine where our money is going, we will allocate it to certain accounts, but still with a holistic view of things. For example, if we have fifty dollars allocated for the electric bill and the electric bill turns out to be only forty dollars, the remaining ten dollars is not an "extra" ten dollars. Rather, it is ten dollars awaiting reallocation. To go out and blow it on something stupid on a spur of the moment whim because it is not ten dollars that we worked for but rather ten "extra" dollars is to really cost ourselves ten dollars. When we have fully achieved our master plan is the soonest that any money will be "extra".

How we spend or invest our money, as well as how we incur debt affects our entire financial outlook. There is only one holistic source of money—you.

In addition to understanding that all money comes from one source, you, and all debt incurred is incurred against one source, you, we have to apply our understanding of this in a consistent manner. What this means is that we cannot go out blowing whatever cash we have on Friday night because we earned it with our attainment of financial goals the previous days of the week. We have to stick to our financial plan in a consistent manner at all times or it just won't work. And finally, we have to be persistent with tenacity. What this means is that we know what is right and we keep doing it, even if we don't see immediate results. Even if we have temporary setbacks. And we do it with tenacity. We don't just go through the motions, but we do it in a manner that actively exemplifies our belief in our plan. So you had a bad day yesterday. So what? Yesterday is gone. Get out there and make things better. Don't do it in a half way manner. If you can do it better, do it. Trying to follow a plan with a negative attitude is a waste of time. After a while you go from negative attitude to just going through the motions to just kind of going through the motions to saying, "forget it" and going on a shopping spree. If you want to succeed, then work to succeed. But if you want to be a wage slave the rest of your life, decide that now and go blow your last cent. Nobody is forcing you to try and succeed. If the call of failure is so enticing, go fail now and stop putting it off. Stop pretending you are something you're not and be a proud failure. Otherwise, embrace your master plan with the vigor it deserves and prove yourself a winner. Holistically realize all your money is your money, consistently follow your master plan to success, and be tenaciously persistent in following this master plan.

The Risk Of Inflation

As we devise our master plan, we have to realize that we require some level of safety in our planning. But as we speak of safety, we must momentarily diverge from our master plan making and address a very real hidden threat to our long term financial well being. We need to face the fact that the term "Safe" can be misleading. When is your money safe? When you have possession of it? Perhaps in a federally insured bank account, maybe even earning a point or so of interest? No. In these "safe" situations, the risk of loss through inflation is greatest. No degree in economics or upper math is required to understand this point. It can be demonstrated very easily. You have $2.00. A gallon of gas cost $2.00. A year later you take your $2.00 that you have kept safe in your possession and buy a gallon of gas. But now gas cost $3.00 per gallon. As surely as you had been robbed or bought stock in a bankrupt company, you lost money. About 33% in this case. The bank paying 2% fares little better; you still end up with $2.04 buying gas at $3.00 per gallon. You still lost about 32%.

Quantify

The beginning of devising our Master Plan is to quantify our needs. By doing this, we have a known destination point and we can start devising our path to get there. Let's start by taking a look at what is required for us to live comfortably every month. Let's imagine $4,000 dollars. Now, we see what kinds of returns we can get on our money once we put it to work. We want enough to cover the inflationary risks, but we don't want to assume that we can get an unrealistically high return; no lottery ticket odds making. At the time of this writing, 7% is a very realistic, even conservative number.

First, we take what we need in a month, in our hypothetical example, $4000.00. Now, we multiply it by 12 for an annual amount—$48,000. Then we divide this annual amount by our estimated rate of return goal, in this case 7%. 7% is .07, so we have 48000/.07. This gives us the result of $685,714.29. Stick with me, we are almost there, and then you will have the key. So then, we add our current debt to this. Let's say that you came up with $25,000 of current debt. The total of these two numbers is $710,714.29. One more math trick. Multiply the total figure of 710,714.29 by 100. Magic number time—71,071,429. There is the mysterious answer to your financial well being.

What this number means is that with this amount of money in pennies, you can pay off your debt and receive enough income via the interest to maintain your current level of living standard (temporarily excluding inflation) without depleting your remaining money (the money left over from the magic number after paying off debt).

Now, of course, that number is only accurate right now. Time enters the equation. If your debt goes up, the number goes up. If your debt goes down, the magic number goes down. Plus, as time goes by, inflation gradually raises all of your expenses, causing the magic number to trickle upward. Taking all of this into account let's us devise somewhat of an accurate magic number. And this process of finding the magic number is what we call Quantification.

The final step in the quantification process, the multiplying by one hundred, is done for a very important purpose. This step provides you with a magic number of minimum units (pennies, remember those little worthless things?) standing between you and financial freedom. Anything you do that brings in any kind of income will produce at least one minimum unit. It is physically impossible for anyone to hand you less than one cent, so we refer to one cent as a minimum unit. A penny is such a miniscule unit, as of this writing, recycling an aluminum can pays a penny, if not more. Now you look at that number and you might be a bit daunted, you might feel even for pennies, it is huge. But here is the kicker, and it is in two parts. First, you have as much of your life as it takes to achieve this number (of course the sooner you get it, the longer you have to enjoy it), and second, we start putting all the little amounts of money that we have been letting freeload and get over with a free ride to work, and they start decreasing the amount we need by bringing in money themselves!

The Grand Deception Of Credit Cards

Now, you might be saying, “Not so fast, buddy. I owe a big chunk on my credit card, maybe five thousand dollars. And I pay maybe one hundred dollars a month, and it only goes down about thirty bucks.” Well, let me explain this to you. In fact, what is happening is the credit card guy is coming up to you and saying: “Look, you owe me five thousand dollars. Give me ALL my money that you owe me and we will be all square. Otherwise, here’s what I’m going to do for you. Give me what you can, at least thirty bucks towards what you owe me, AND pay me off with another seventy bucks cash RIGHT NOW FOR ME, and I’ll give you another month to come up with my money”. So no, you didn’t pay one hundred dollars on your credit card, you paid thirty dollars on your credit card, and BOUGHT another month of time for seventy dollars! Yes, you spent seventy dollars without even noticing it! Ain’t credit grand?

More On The Power Of Quantifying

Let's discuss just a bit more the principle of quantifying. If you know that you need a lot of money, that is an abstract number. What is a lot of money? Depends on who you ask and when you ask them. If however, you know that you need three million dollars, you know what you need. Three million dollars and one cent is more than you need. Two million is a lot of money, but not enough. Quantify your needs. Accept the requirements and work on it. Don't chase abstract amounts, it is futile. You have to know how much you need and what you are going to do with it when you get it. It does not mean that the amount won't change, but it does put a finite number into the equation that can be worked with.

Money And Time Have Value And The Amount Of Risk Also Affects Value

Investors are familiar with these two concepts, as are banks and other entities engaged in loaning money. When you borrow money, what you are doing is renting it. The longer you rent it for, the more the rent will cost. This rent is the interest. The longer the money is rented for (loaned to you) the more money in interest you will pay. In addition, the riskier you are perceived to be (credit risk) the higher the interest rate you will have to pay. This is not all bad. Actually, it is very good. It is good because these rules work both ways. The longer you loan money for, the higher the interest rate, and the riskier the investment, the greater the return.

People Invest Less In A Month Than They Will Spend On A Friday Night And Still Expect It To Support Their Retirement

It is really amazing the number of people that put away twenty-five dollars a month and really think that their financial future is assured. This is crazy. If someone puts aside twenty-five dollars a month, that is three hundred dollars a year. Think about it a minute, if it costs three hundred dollars a week now to live comfortably, how are you going to live on an investment of that amount per year?

Stupid Non-Investments

You can twist the definition of an investment to include anything up to and including the dog droppings in the back yard. We are not going to play the word game. We are going to establish something right here and right now. For our usage, an investment is something that a reasonable person can purchase with their money and expect to get their original money and a profit returned when they sell the investment.

For instance, a person can put one hundred dollars into a bank account with a four percent annual yield and expect to get their original one hundred dollars back (the amount of the original investment) plus four dollars (the profit) at the end of the year. This is an investment. On the other hand, a person that buys an SUV for twenty thousand dollars, finances eighty percent of it at fifteen percent interest for five years, pays three hundred dollars average per year on maintenance, plus fuel, plus insurance, plus incidental damage, plus the loss of value from the mileage applied every time the vehicle is driven does not have an investment. He has an expensive toy. And, unless he has already discovered the road to financial freedom and has made some mighty strides down it, he has a money pit and a nightmare. Don't get me wrong—if you can really afford this extravagance using our definition of afford which is coming up shortly (which you can't, since you had to finance eighty percent of it at fifteen percent), and it is something you have on your list of most important things in life (OK, not a real requirement if you have really, really, really made it big), go for it. But if you fell into it because someone told you that you look good in it or, heaven forbid, that it was a great investment, the only financial freedom you helped to achieve was, unfortunately, someone else's.

Let's look at an imaginary story. About a guy named Dave. You can change his name to anything you like, Dave is imaginary, he won't mind. Dave has a beautiful electric table saw. Dave carries it with him everywhere he goes. OK, actually it is too big for Dave to carry anywhere. Dave pays two big men to carry the saw everywhere Dave goes. The saw is perfect for a true wood working guru. With the right skills, a craftsman can do miracles with this saw. You might suspect that that is why Dave has it carried everywhere he goes. Many people that don't know Dave take one look at the saw and come to this conclusion. They are wrong. Dave isn't a wood worker. Dave has a hard time recognizing wood whenever he is confronted with it. But Dave will tell you, he doesn't want there ever to come a day when he needs his table saw and doesn't have it.

Dave had a friend once that borrowed the saw. By Dave having the saw, it saved the friend twenty dollars that he would have had to pay to rent a saw. Of course, this saved twenty dollars did not begin to pay for the saw, it barely paid for the two men that carried it to the friend's house.

Pretty silly story, isn't it? But this seems to be the exact attitude that people display when buying a new vehicle. They never haul anything, but they have to have a huge truck, just in case the day comes when they need to haul something. Or when a friend needs to haul something. Never mind that the daily rental on a truck comes nothing close to the payment on this puppy, and with the wasted gas of driving a large truck everywhere they go they could hire a moving crew to make the seldom haul, they maintain their peace of mind by having a truck.

There is a similar mind set in many SUV owners as well. I am sure you have seen them, or know them, or might even be them. These are the folks that seldom have more than one passenger, consider a dirt road to be "out in the boonies", and the closest they have ever come to even thinking about military service is getting up on the Fourth of July, but they need an SUV. And it better be a big one. And raised, God, we can't have it the same height as everybody else, what if we need to drive over a fire hydrant? And four wheel drive. That is a must. The last time it rained, the road got wet! And to make the deal sweeter still, let's get one that the military uses for something; that must mean that it is good for everything. And if it's not one the military uses, let's at least make it look like we imagine something the military uses would look like. Because that's what enhances the vehicles' "get me to work and back" ability—appearance.

What You Can Afford Does Not Mean What Payment You Can Afford

In our society of instant gratification, being able to afford something is being able to afford the payment. No. Being able to afford something in our strictest sense means being able to pay the full amount at the time of purchase and never missing the money.

Otherwise, we must determine if it is a necessity in our master plan, or is it absolutely realistically necessary, and if so, are we going about the purchase in the most intelligent manner.

For example, a replacement vehicle may be realistically necessary. The type of vehicle however, is not determined by our master plan (as in, we do not live for the day that we have a truck, which will make our life complete and allow us to await the angels to take us to our just reward and eternal rest). So then, the first thing that we do is we come to terms with the fact that this is an expense. Nothing more. Our prime concern with this expense is how to minimize its impact on our master plan. To achieve this, we consider key points such as the initial cost of the vehicle, the cost of the money to purchase this vehicle (both in the terms of if we have to borrow the money, or, if we are paying cash, the loss of income from the money that we are parting with.) Then we have to look at operating costs, both fuel and maintenance. Does it get great gas mileage but cost four times as much to be repaired? Something to consider. Does it suck very little gas but cost a ghastly premium because of this fact? After looking at the facts, the fuel savings may not equal or exceed the initial increase in cost.

Look At Where Your Money Goes

Many times, just analyzing a purchase with the light of reason can save a good sum of money. Impulse purchases at the store can put a hefty dent in your personal finance.

Next up the ladder of waste is substituting quality where it really doesn't matter. When you go to buy something, ask yourself if the quality that you are buying is best in the long run, or if this purchase is probably a single use item and the higher level of quality is probably not needed. For instance, for many years I have worked on computers. For this work, I need a tool set that is small. High quality is not necessarily a requirement for a couple of reasons. First, seldom are the screws and assorted hardware on with any degree of tightness—generally, if I actually have a tool that will fit the screw, bolt, nut, or whatever, it will do the job. Secondly, I loose tools. A lot.

Now then, when putting together my tool kits, there is very little upward limit to how much I can spend. How much do I spend? A couple of bucks. No, not through specialty wholesalers, but through run of the mill discount stores. Cheap, made wherever tools. Of the right size for working on computers. Not for working on cars, or stereos or TV's, not air conditioners or small appliances. Those are not the things that I work on. I work on computers.

Cash is King—The King is Dead

It is amazing in this day and age (even in the day and age of decades ago) that so many people think that all cash is the way to go. In certain circumstances, I will admit that cash is king. Flea markets, yard sales, estate sales, things of this nature often demand a need for cash. What this means is that at times we will need to be able to easily obtain cash. It does not mean that we devote our lives to a pure cash existence.

I have come across quite a few people that maintain a pure cash existence because they are afraid of the responsibilities of having a checking account. They pay everything they can in cash, and when they can't, they buy a money order. These people often spout the fact that they are afraid of bouncing a check, and if they don't write checks, they cannot bounce checks. This is like never getting out of diapers. If you never embrace potty training, you will never have an accident. Sound ridiculous? It is.

Let's examine a bit closer this whole cash mentality. First, when you pay with cash, the only way you have to prove that you paid is by getting a receipt. If you fail to get a receipt and later there is a dispute, there is no way to prove that you paid. Even if you do get a receipt but later can't find it, you still can't prove that you paid. To make matters worse, it is as if you never paid AND your money is gone.

When you pay with a credit card, a debit card, or a check, there is always a paper trail to follow. The term "paper trail" scares so many people unnecessarily. The effect is very similar to people's excessive compulsion with security and passwords on computers. The movies have portrayed the "paper trail" as being the key piece of evidence that even the most genius of evildoers cannot overcome. This "paper trail" leads to their ultimate demise and lands them in jail. Guess what? The "paper trail" did not put them behind bars, the crime the trail led to did. No crime, no jail. What are you trying to hide?

Nobody really cares how much you spent at the store last weekend, or how much your cable bill was last month. Nobody but you. And you should really care. The only way to have control of our finances is to know what is going on. In this area, what you don't know CAN hurt you. A lot.

But being able to prove that we paid for something is only the beginning. Banking service offers many, many advantages over cash. Think about it. If banks and checks and credit cards offered only an alternative to cash with no advantages, would the banking business have not only survived but thrived over the past hundreds of years?

When you deal with people in the business world and you deal strictly in cash and money orders, it sends up an immediate red flag that there is something off kilter with you. The astute businessperson understands that you may simply be eccentric. But he will also consider the fact that perhaps you have trouble managing your finances, or maybe that your money is not obtained legally and so you are trying to avoid leaving a paper trail.

You may wonder what difference it makes. I will explain it to you—it means a lot.

Let's assume that I am your landlord and that you are paying your rent with cash or a money order. The first thing that I have to wonder is why you are not paying with a check. It could be that you have bounced so many checks in the past that you no longer have a bank account. Why you bounced them is not important to me. What it does mean is that you are not reliable. True, by paying me with a money order I know that it will not bounce. But it makes me wonder if you will be able to pay next month's rent. I have to wonder about your ability to manage your finances in a responsible manner. It is true that I would probably rather not get a money order on time next month than get a bad check that is on time. But that is like saying I would rather die painlessly than painfully. In truth, I would rather not die at all. I have all of these concerns if you are paying with cash, plus more. With cash I have to also wonder if you are getting the money legitimately or if you are getting the money in an illegal manner. What difference does it make to me? It makes a big difference. As soon as I accept your money, I am involved.

Now, maybe you are a nice, above board, outstanding citizen that has never not paid a bill on time in your life. And maybe you pay everything in cash because Grandma always preached about the hardships of the great depression because of the banks failing. Guess what? I don't care. I am in business, and there are too many people out there for me to waste time on those who are at best eccentric and at worst more trouble that they are worth.

And it piles up on you even further. OK, I don't want your business, but there are plenty of other people that do. But this should send up a red flag to you. Why do they want your business? There is a chance that they are just nice guys that know what it is like to be having hard times. They will take your business. Until they get burned enough times. Or put out of business.

Or, perhaps, their being nice guys has little or nothing to do with it. Maybe they realize that you are limited to where you can go, and that is what their business is built on. They realize that you are a riskier customer than the average, and so their prices are inflated accordingly. More risk, more reward. Now you are paying a premium for your cash-only tendencies. Is it so important for you to stay away from banks that you would pay good money to do so? Some might say yes, that at least there is no chance of high credit card interest or bounced check fees. Rubbish. You have control over both of these items. Pay your credit card off at the end of every month. If there is still a charge of any kind, you need a different credit card. And to really twist up a phrase, "banks don't bounce checks, people bounce checks". Yes, I am aware bank errors happen. It is rare. Also, if bank errors are happening more than very, very rarely, and they really are bank errors, you have the wrong bank. Move your money.

But wait, it gets worse. Let's return to our rent scenario and you are dealing with one of the two specimens outlined above. With the nice guy, if he gets burned enough, he is going to be put out of business. You have to move. With the second fellow, if he builds up enough of a business on flakes and they don't come through, you have to move. Or worse, he gets closed down for involvement with illegal activities. Guess what? You have to move.

None of these scenarios seems in your best interest. And, there's more. So everything goes like in a perfect world; the landlord doesn't get closed down, you don't have to move. Great. But what about the other tenants that are paying in cash for some of the less desirable reasons that we outlined above? Well, what if a few of them are paying in cash because they cannot balance their finances? No bounced checks, that's true. But instead of bad checks, the landlord receives either late payment or nothing. How is the landlord going to stay in business with those types of interruptions to his cash flow? Charge everybody extra so there is enough money to cover the bad times. So now you are paying more rent because neighbor lady can't manage to pay her rent on time. Not good.

And what about neighbor man or neighbor lady paying in cash because the income is less than legit? Can you think of an entrepreneurial endeavor they might be involved in that you don't mind them doing from where you live? If they are growing the money, either figuratively or literally, I don't want them doing it anywhere around where I live. And if they are doing it through the resell of stolen goods, I definitely don't want them living near me; they may decide that I have some nice merchandise for their resell business!

I briefly mentioned earlier that keeping track of your finances is another key factor in using banking services. Let's expand on that. One of the horrible things that happens to cash is that it as it is used, it turns into change. Change, as everyone knows, is worthless. Look on the street. Whenever somebody wants your money, they will ask for "extra change you don't want". What is "extra" about it and why would I not want it? Apparently, as soon as cash becomes change, it is extra. And when it is extra, you don't want it. I have actually seen people throw away change because it is extra and they don't want it. I have seen them heave it as far away as they physically can, and I have seen them accumulate it in the car ashtray until the ashtray is full and then dump it in a nice little stack in the parking lot.

When I first entered the Army in 1981, I would pick up this discarded change. This brought immense amusement to the discarders. They eventually progressed from throwing pennies and nickels and dimes to quarters and half dollars and dollar coins because it was so amusing to see me pick up the coins. Imagine, someone bending over to pick up money, and not just "good" money, but change!

It is becoming more and more widespread for the average person not to look at change as real money. The following story is real. It happened just the other day. It has happened in one form or another a number of times, but this most recent occurrence has happened recent enough that I can set it to paper with an unerring memory. Very simply, I was in my bank making a deposit. I laid a check and four pennies on the counter in front of the teller and said, "Deposit, please". The teller picked up the check, read the account number off of the back, entered it into her computer, did whatever else these tellers do on the computer to make a deposit, and then said, "Oh, did you want to deposit the four cents also?" Why else would I have laid out four pennies and a check and said the words "Deposit, please" if I did not intend to actually deposit the four pennies?

In the past, I have had the teller (different tellers each time) make the deposit and leave the change laying there unaccounted for, and when I ask about it they look at me blankly and say that they didn't know I wanted the change deposited too. And I have had the teller take the change with the check as if depositing it, but the deposit not reflect the change. This one I did not catch until I had left the bank. Bye, bye money.

And what about the people that ask for "extra" change? Imagine it in a different context. Imagine if when you went to pick up your paycheck that you had worked all week for, you were asked how much of the money that was owed to you that you wished to receive, and how much was just extra. If it's not extra when you are working for it, why is it extra when it is change and you are giving it away?

Project #2—Pennies in a Jar: Watch Them Grow!

This next project is a bit of tongue-in-cheek fun, so you might want to read the entire procedure before starting. OK, you have been warned, let's go! First, round up all of the loose change that you can find. Now count how much of it there is. Write down the total and put this number in a safe place where we can be sure to refer to it later.

Now, find a jar with a lid that will hold all of the change. Put the change in the jar. Now put on the lid. For good measure, wrap some tape around the lid so that we are sure that none of the coins get out. Great. Now put the jar in a safe place where it will not be tampered with by anybody. Wait about a week or so. Maybe three weeks if you have the patience. Now go and retrieve the jar. Peel off the tape. Open the lid. Count the coins. Compare the total to the total that we wrote down at the beginning of this project. If you did everything right, the number is the same! Guess what? Money doesn't grow just because you put it in a jar and forget about it!

That was a bit of fun, but seriously, it is exactly what many people do. They don't throw their money into the air or dump it out with the trash, but they do pour it into a jar or can or some other enclosure and set it aside where it not only doesn't grow, but it actually looses buying power through the erosion of inflation.

Preserving Your Credit Score

This topic should be a no brainer, but for some reason, the smoke and mirrors confuses people. If you owe someone money and don't pay it, in their eyes you have stolen their money. Not the best way to get a glowing recommendation when asking for a referral. And that is what a credit score or credit rating is: a referral.

Often I see commercials on TV telling me about how if I have too much credit card debt (Hmm, how much is too much? If it is more than I want to pay back is it too much?) They can "work with" my creditors and get the interest reduced, the late fees forgiven, maybe even the principle reduced! How? Well, the commercials throw out terms like "secret government programs" and "special relationships with lenders". According to the commercial, I have borrowed so much money for a certain percentage (often based on my credit history up to that point), and they are going to arrange it so that I really don't have to pay that percentage, I don't have to pay the late fees for those monthly payments that I skipped, I don't even have to pay back all the money that I borrowed! And when you use a credit card, that is what you are doing. You are borrowing money to make a purchase. The nice TV or radio commercial people are going to do all this for me, and it won't even mess up my credit! I don't think so. I think the miracle goes something like this:

> Miracle Worker: *"Ah, yes sir, I am calling from Miracle Debt Relief on behalf of our client, Joe Deadbeat. We need to work with you to develop a plan so that Mr. Deadbeat can pay you what he owes you."*
>
> Fellow About To Be Screwed Out Of What You Owe Him: *"Ah, well, we already have a plan. He agreed to it when he borrowed the money."*
>
> Miracle Worker: *"Yes, well, the plan is now null and void ..."*
>
> Fellow About To Be Screwed Out Of What You Owe Him: *"It is? Why?"*
>
> Miracle Worker: *"Well, first of all, you are charging our client way too much interest."*
>
> Fellow About To Be Screwed Out Of What You Owe Him: *"But it is the interest that he agreed to. And with his credit, we were being charitable at that rate!"*
>
> Miracle Worker: *"Well, he didn't know what he was agreeing to. Plus, his credit record was not his fault. How can he be expected to pay every bill that he receives? We think you are asking way too much of our client."*

Fellow About To Be Screwed Out Of What You Owe Him: *"Either way, why would I be willing to make these negotiations with you and your client?"*

Miracle Worker: *"Oh, you really have no choice. If you don't play ball with us, our client won't ever pay you anything. He might go bankrupt, or he may simply let you sue and get a judgment. I understand that judgments can be used for wallpaper if you accumulate enough of them. Either way, actually getting any money will be out of the question."*

Fellow About To Be Screwed Out Of What You Owe Him (beginning to realize that he is being robbed and still thinking he can manage to salvage something): *"OK, so if I rework the interest you can insure that your client pays what he owes?"*

Miracle Worker: *"Not so fast. You have some late fees and missed payment fees listed here ..."*

Fellow About To Be Screwed Out Of What You Owe Him: *"Those are legitimate charges for when your client either was late with his payment or didn't make it at all!"*

Miracle Worker: *"Yea, we really don't worry about legitimacy."*

Fellow About To Be Screwed Out Of What You Owe Him (Fully realizing and resigned to the fact that he has been shafted): *"OK, what do I need to do to get something out of your client?"*

Miracle Worker: *"I am so happy that we could work together on this matter! We feel that if you will drop all late fees, reduce the interest by seventy percent, and waive sixty percent of the debt, our client can repay the remainder of what he owes you, say, over the next five years?"*

Yes, you might get a debt reduced, but if you actually think the guy you just screwed is going to give you a glowing recommendation, you have got to be kidding! Kiss your credit rating good-bye!

Dealing With The Bank And How It Should Be

Before you really need your bank, you should see how they treat you and if they deserve your business. Always looking to improve my financial position, a few years ago I decided to see about taking out an equity loan on my house and paying off all credit card debt. Crunching the numbers, it gave me a better payment, a better interest, a sooner payoff, and allowed enough of a remainder for my upcoming honeymoon. The numbers said it was a really good deal, but I didn't know if I was totally sold. Having credit card debt was one thing, but having a debt secured by my house was another thing entirely. Plus, to be quite honest, I did not totally trust my bank, having never needed to rely on them before.

I will be honest, I was not comfortable asking for a loan, and I let the bank know it. If I had been talked down to or treated anywhere near as bad as I would be treated at a later date when I forgot about my friendly banker and gave a local mortgage company a try, I would have walked out. I went in and told the bank that I was interested in an equity loan on my house, and that I wanted it to be of a certain amount. No more, no less. If it was a problem, I was not interested. If there were any hoops to jump through, forget it.

Truthfully, we were finished and I thought we were just talking. The bank person informed me that the soonest I could get the money was something like ten days or two weeks due to a state law, I should bring in proof of insurance on the property and the previous year's income tax (one year), the rate was such and such, the payment so and so, the term was what I had asked for, the principle what I wanted. I said it sounded great, what did we need to do to get started? I signed once or twice, and it was a done deal.

Yes, that is how it is supposed to be when you deal with your bank from a position of strength, i.e. good credit, control of your debt, available credit, established income, etc.

As an added bonus, I later received a standard letter from the bank explaining the factors affecting the loan that I had applied for. One of the factors had been my credit score of 830. I had no idea what this meant. I knew I should have good credit, for years I had been paying my bills ahead of time, reducing my debt when possible, and just doing the day-to-day things that are right. I searched the net, and it showed that 850 was normally the high. Cool.

Putting It All Together: Good Credit, Financial Knowledge, Common Sense

Time for a true-life tale of just what can happen when you don't pay attention to the rules of the game. And also how the game can be salvaged when you are prepared. As my wedding approached a while back, my wife-to-be and I knew that we would need a larger place to live. I had a house, full, and she had a house, also full. The wedding was scheduled for the early part of December, and we finally located a house that fit all requirements (size, price, condition, location, etc.) in about October. Being pressed for time, I made my first mistake: I rationalized that it must be easier and quicker to just use the mortgage company that was preferred by the builder and in the same building as the builder, instead of going to my own personal banker. I had taken an equity loan on my house the year before through my bank to eliminate all credit card debt, and I knew how painless things (should) would be. Oh, boy, was I wrong.

My agent called me in the afternoon and gave me the name and number of the person to talk to at the mortgage company. I then called the number, and the lady let me know how happy they were to have my business, scheduled my appointment for the next day, and listed out the reams and reams of paperwork—previous years (multiple) tax filings, bank statements, etc.—that I should bring with me. I was very pleasant with the lady, still mislead into thinking that we were working together. I let her know that I would have all of the paperwork together. I also let her know how on my most recent credit report my score had been an 830. The woman acted like she had no idea what that meant, and, oh yes, there would be a fifty dollar interview fee. No, I told the woman, I don't pay interview fees or any other such nonsense charges. She said yes, that it was required, so I thanked her for her time and told her that I would not be there the next day.

I should have stopped right there and just gone to my bank. But no, stupidity breeds masochism. I called my real estate agent and recounted what had occurred.

The real estate agent called me back the next morning and said all was straightened out, the mortgage company had waived the fee and would see me at 11:00 that morning. I was an idiot and agreed to be there.

At about 10:55 that morning I walked into the mortgage company and told the girl at the front desk that I was there to meet with the mortgage officer for my 11:00 appointment. The girl's attitude quickly let me know that she really did not care who I was or why I was there, they were doing me a favor by seeing me, whenever that happened to be. She handed me a clipboard with a huge stack of papers to be filled out and pointed me to a plastic chair. Well, I knew from my previous experience with my own bank that I had not had to fill out a clipboard full of paperwork, and now being told to sit and wait after the incident with the interview charge, I wasn't filling out any stack of papers by hand.

Apparently my time was not important to anyone but me. 11:00 came and went, as did 11:30. The whole time I sat in the plastic chair and watched the show going on in the loan officer's office. It was very clear that she was in no hurry. She sat there patiently listening to the loan applicant explain why his car had been repossessed the most recent time. Another warning sign. Why am I waiting on someone to explain their repossessions, and why am I doing business with a company that expects me to wait while they deal with bad credit applicants?

At 11:35 I stood up to leave. The loan officer noticed my pending escape and invited me in while shaking hands and saying goodbye to Mr. "I don't even pay my car payment—loan me money".

The next hour and a half was a nightmare. We reviewed my previous years' income tax returns and my bank records. In addition, I had brought in paperwork from my investment company showing my investments. The loan officer looked at this completely lost. I explained that those were investment in mutual funds, that I did not keep the bulk of my money in the checking account where it was not making any money.

She was still confused and asked me if the mutual funds were like a stock or something. I told her yes, they were something like that. She flipped papers and did figuring, shook her head and finally told me how difficult it was going to be to get me financed, but she would try.

I still didn't understand why it was going to be so difficult. My last bank loan had not been difficult at all, and now I had even less debt and more money than I did then, and was still sporting perfect credit. Of course, now I know the whole thing was an act to convince ignorant little me that I was getting a good rate when in fact what I was getting was raped.

A true thespian till the end, the loan officer finally wrapped up the performance by telling me that it would take about a week and a half or so, but she felt confident she could get my loan slipped through. The interest rate that she felt confident she could get for me I felt was a bit inflated to say the least. But you have to give it to her, she was thorough; she slid over a stack of papers for me to sign to "get the loan started". Buried in the middle was a form saying that I agreed to pay the fifty-dollar interview fee that we had already discussed the day before. I pulled out that piece of paper and handed it to her unsigned, and she just looked at me blankly and said, "You don't want to sign this one?" I said "no". The hour and a half was one of the longest of my life.

I left to continue with what was left of the day. Luck finally broke through where it should not have had to. I should have not wasted the morning, and I should have had enough sense to know what to do next without counting on luck. But I didn't, so luck had to come through for me.

I went to a client that had called while I was waiting to go into the loan office, and then I went to my bank to make a deposit. I had a splitting headache from the abuse of the morning, so I grabbed a cup of coffee hoping that would help.

Just on a wild impulse, as I was leaving I walked over to a cubicle. I asked the woman in the cubicle if she had a second, told her that I was trying to buy a house and had just had one of the most aggravating mornings of my life. She asked me how much the house was, my account number, my social security number, did some key clicking on her computer, and before I could either drink my coffee or sit down, she said I was approved. I was having a dense moment, so I asked her what that meant. She said it meant that I was approved, and that if I wanted to do it, have a seat and we could print out the papers. I told her that I had the stack of papers that the mortgage company had required out in the car and that I could go get them, but she said that was not necessary.

By the time my small cup of coffee was gone, the loan process was completed, I had my packet, and I had an interest rate that was lower than the one offered by the mortgage company that morning. Lower by whole number percentage points, I might add.

The remainder of the home purchase went fairly smoothly with one exception. As a final declaration of how much in bed the builder was with the mortgage company, after I had notified my real estate agent that my bank was handling the financing, she called me back that the builder was no longer willing to pay the closing costs as agreed upon.

His quote was something like "Anyone that can get their own financing doesn't need me to pay their closing costs". I don't remember the exact outcome of that, but it really didn't matter—my bank had already offered to pick up most of the tab themselves.

Two Quick Ways To Improve Your Position

In Part II we will be getting into the somewhat dry but necessary topic of establishing an accounting system. So to help cut through the dryness, here are two very easy ways to better your financial position very quickly. They don’t sound like much just reading through them, but they do indeed help when they are put into practice.

Pay The Bill When It Is Received, Not When It Is Due!

How do we get started? You've climbed down into the pit of debt and now are ready to start climbing up the ladder of financial freedom. But where to begin? Where is the first rung of this ladder, so to speak?

Start moving up the date when you pay your bills. Get the concept in your head that the bill in not due by the due date, it is due to go back out the day it is received. This way, your back isn't up against the wall and the first time that something unforeseen occurs, you have a little breathing room.

We prepare for the bills in advance, we put the money into the appropriate "account"—phone, electric, water, and the like in the utilities account, etc.—and when the bill is received, we pull the money from the appropriate holding account and pay the bill. The actual account level information will be discussed on Part II.

Insurance Bills

The next step we look at is the different insurance bills. If you have auto insurance, car insurance, or anything like this, we want to work to the point where we are paying the entire premium amount when it is due, not in monthly payments. Take a look at your next insurance bill. It will say something like: To pay entire premium for six months, remit $180.00. For three months, please remit $94.00. For one month, please remit a payment of $23.00.

Looking at the monthly payment, the first thing that comes to mind is "Wow, it is a lot easier to pay twenty-three bucks a month than one hundred eighty dollars in one shot!" But if we look closer at our example, we see that we are paying eighteen dollars for that convenience. Not bad, eighteen bucks, six months, not bad. Or is it? Well, first, in this example, eighteen dollars is actually ten percent of the original principle of $180.00. Ten percent. That's rough to get on a sure thing. But it gets better. That was ten percent on the original amount, but that amount is decreasing monthly. And the term is only six months. Without getting too technical, the sweet deal turns out to be more like a twenty percent plus annual hosing! Imagine how small your magic number would be if you could collect a sure thing twenty percent annual return!

So how do we get out of this trap of convenience? Hands on instruction, that's what the book is about, right? Well, here it is.

Identify one insurance bill. Continue to pay the bill in whatever increment (monthly, bi-monthly, whatever) that you have been paying, but look and see how much the full premium is.

Add some additional on to this amount, since there is no guarantee that it won't increase next time around. If you know it is going to increase (maybe you got a ticket—bad, bad, bad), don't put your head in the sand. Face the reality, and add more than a little to this figure. Add a good-sized chunk. However much you add, try to add enough that you honestly believe that there is no way it can go up that much.

This is our target amount to start saving. Start setting this amount aside now and make every effort to reach the goal amount by the beginning of the next premium cycle. Now, if you are on payment six of six, this might not be too realistic, in which case we would target the second premium to come. Perhaps even the third, if funds are that tight.

Once we reach our goal and have the money set aside for the full premium, begin paying the insurance in full every premium period. Then, every month instead of sending in money to the insurance company (the monthly bill is already paid, remember?) set the money aside to apply to the insurance premium the next time it is due. Instant savings of whatever the interest they were charging is! Plus, instead of scraping up the money when the bill is received, the money is already there, maybe (hopefully?) even earning some interest of its own while it waits!

On Taxes

Let's touch on taxes. In a phrase, the phrase would be "Pay Them". All the money in the world will not do you any good if all your assets are frozen and you are sitting in jail. I believe on this matter the same as on other similar matters such as law and medicine—get the services of a professional. And as your wealth grows, a full time professional. By full time professional I do not necessarily mean full time in your employ, but rather someone that practices the profession full time as a profession, not somebody that does taxes three months out of the year and folds shirts at the local clothing store the other nine months. You want somebody who is about taxes and accounting, not somebody who is about picking up some extra money on evenings and weekends during the tax season and maybe bartending the rest of the year. This is one area where cost is my least consideration. As with my lawyer, I am more interested in finding someone that knows what they are doing, are available, professional, and accurate. Especially accurate. Experience helps, as well. I do not perform my own surgery, I don't defend myself in court, and I don't do my own taxes. There are other areas as well that if: a) I don't know what I am doing, or b) I don't want to do it, or c) it is not worth my time, which has value, I hire a professional.

A good rule of thumb to consider is to simply ask what is the likelihood of something going wrong, and how much will the additional cost be to hire a professional to fix things after that something goes wrong. Now compare that cost to the cost of having it done right the first time by a professional. If you are honest and accurate in your assessment, you should be able to determine if it would be in your best interest to hire a professional.

Computers

Nothing that we are going to do in this book requires you to have or know how to use a computer. Just like in the modern world you are not strictly required to know how to operate a phone or a car, nor are you required to possess shoes. However, you will be facing a definite disadvantage if you don't. This is the twenty-first century. Computers have been with us a lot longer than the average person might realize; I bought my first home computer in 1985. As of this writing, that was twenty-one years ago. But I took my first computer class in 1979. Again, as of this writing, twenty-seven years ago. And at that year in 1979, the computer had already progressed to the point where the class that I took was taught in high school and open to anyone that signed up. Computers are tools, and not using one is nothing but a way to make your life less productive and success harder to achieve.

PART II

A System For Success

The System

In this section, I will show you a step-by-step approach to the foundation of my system, in both a computerized and non-computerized method.

The cornerstone of my system is knowledge and control of our finances. To control our money, we have to know what we have, and what every penny is allocated for. We do this through a sub-account system. Understanding this system is critical to our success. If you don't understand this system, 90 percent of this book will be useless to you. For that reason, I am going to take it slow. Not only slow, but also at times you may think that I am being too repetitive. If so, that is great. You understand the concept. But bear with me. Even if you grasp the idea, further examples should serve to make it clearer. If you don't grasp it at first, don't worry. I plan on explaining it over a few times in a couple of different ways so that everyone should be able to grasp the concept without too much hair pulling.

In our first example, let's say that we have two hundred and fifty dollars cash. From this two hundred and fifty dollars we make three stacks. The first stack has seventy dollars. The second stack has one hundred dollars, and the third stack has eighty dollars. On each stack, we place a piece of paper with a label written on it. The first says "Gasoline", the second says "Food", and the third says "Electric". We still have two hundred and fifty dollars. But we also have a stack for where each portion of the two hundred and fifty dollars is supposed to go. Each stack represents a sub-account, and the total of the three stacks represents our checking account.

Let's visualize it another way. Suppose we have a box. A shoebox. Into this shoebox, we place three cans. Empty dog food cans with the lids cut off. Now we label each of the three cans. "Electricity" for one, "Food" for another, and "Gasoline" for the third. In the first can that we labeled "Gasoline" we place seventy dollars. In the can labeled "Food" we place one hundred dollars, and in the can labeled "Electricity" we place eighty dollars. Each can represents a sub-account, and the box represents our checking account. We still have two hundred and fifty dollars in the box. It makes no difference how we shuffle around the money in the cans, the box will always have the same amount of money. The only way the box has less money is if we take money out of the box. The only way the box has more money is if we add money to the box. No matter how we move money around from can to can, the amount of money in the box remains the same. If we take all the money out of the first and third can and put it all in the second can, the box still has the same amount of money. No matter how we move it around inside the box, the amount of money in the box does not change.

If we take it to the next level we begin to deal with bank accounts. Let us say that we have a checking account with $250.00 in it. One bank account, $250.00. Seventy dollars of this we plan on using for gasoline to get to work next week, one hundred dollars for food, and eighty dollars for the electric bill that is due tomorrow. Well, from this we can identify a need for three sub-accounts: Electricity (or Utilities), Fuel (or Automotive) and Food (or Operating).

The first rule of our process is that there is a main sub-account that all transactions come into or go out of. This is our Transfer account. Our transfer account acts like an index. We can easily look at the transactions in this account and review all money that has gone into or come out of the account. Think of it as a doorway. For money to get into our checking account, it has to go in the doorway, and for it to get out of our checking account, it has to go through the doorway. We need a name for the transfer account. I like to call the transfer account something that will let me know what physical account it is the transfer account for. In this case, since the physical account is the checking account, I would call the transfer account "Checking".

Now, we have to keep out thinking straight. We have one bank account, a checking account. Within the checking account, we have four sub-categories. We have Checking, Utilities, Automotive, and Operating. These categories do not exist anywhere outside of our imagination and whatever kind of system that we use to keep track of our finances. The bank has no record of these categories, our bank statement will not reflect the categories. The categories by themselves do not increase or decrease the amount of money that we have in the account. Physically they do not exist! The categories are a tool to help us keep track of our money.

We can run our sub-account system either through a computer, or by hand. With a computer, I find the easiest way to track my money is with personal finance software.

There are a couple of personal finance software packages out there for not too much money, and a few free ones as well. Computers will often come with a free version of a financial manager software package. This is the way the I would recommend tracking your money. However, I did track my money for many years with just a spreadsheet, so that is definitely possible.

Even without a computer the system can be used. It is a lot more work, but it is possible. What you use to keep track of your money is not as important as understanding the system. It's sort of like golf clubs. Until you learn to hit the ball, the price of the clubs are not going to do much to improve your game.

In a manual system, we will need as many check ledgers as we have sub-accounts, including our "main" transfer account. Keep in mind, there is nothing sacred about naming conventions. As long as you understand the system and it works for you, you can name your accounts whatever you choose. Know also that I have changed my naming method through the years, as well as added and deleted accounts as the necessity arose. I will be sharing with you the result of many years of fine-tuning of my own system, but you use what works best for you. Just keep in mind a few basic rules:

1. Only one sub-account for each "real" account is used for money coming in or money going out.

2. Name your sub-accounts in such a manner that you can instantly without a doubt identify which "real" account it is a sub-account of. Although right now we may be so far in debt that stone broke would be an improvement, we don't plan on staying that way.

And, where a single checking account meets our needs and more right now, it won't for long. Among other things, a checking account does not pay the return that our money deserves, because our money, like our time, has value. So then, we will need to designate what real account each sub-account is a sub of. For Example, all checking sub-accounts might start with a C—. In this case, you might have the following:

C—Checking
C—Utilities
C—Automotive
C—Operating

3. Every transaction of any type gets recorded.

To start our project, we are going to create our four sub-accounts (Automotive, Operating, Utilities, and our transfer account, Checking.) So then, we have one "real" account, which we will refer to as Checking. And we have four sub-accounts. Now don't get confused. The real account is called Checking, and there is also a sub-account called C—Checking. We can always identify a sub-account by the fact that it has a leading indicator, in this case, the C and the dash. If you find having the real account and a sub-account having the same name to be too confusing, change it. The sub-account in this instance could always be called something like C—Transfer. For our example we are going to stick with C—Checking, but you use whatever is best for you.

Now then, our four sub accounts are:

C—Checking
C—Utilities
C—Operating

C—Automotive

To do this on the computer, we go into our financial software and we set up a bank account (as per the instructions that came with the software) and we name it C—Checking. If the software asks what financial institution this account is held at, I normally answer "none" or "it is not held at a financial institution", since it is not a "real" account. We show our beginning balance of $250.00. Now we set up another account. This account we name C—Utilities with an opening balance of $00.00, since it has no money in it. All accounts except for the main transfer account (in this case, C—Checking) start with a balance of zero. All funding for these accounts must pass through the transfer account. We set up the two remaining sub-accounts, C—Operating and C—Automotive, in the same manner. Now we go into our main transfer account of C—Checking (or whatever you named yours), and we transfer $70.00 to our C—Automotive account. It is a Transfer, the Payee is C—Automotive, the payment is the amount, and the category is the account it is being transferred to. You may include a memo if there is something to say that will help you understand the transaction when you look back on it.

Click the enter button, and the transaction is complete. Now repeat it for the $80.00 transfer to C—Utilities and the $100.00 transfer to C—Operating. This leaves your transfer account with a balance of $0.00. You have no spending money, but you do have the money for the fuel, electricity, and food that you need.

Now we reverse the process to pay any bill or use the money (hopefully for what it is intended). In the case of the electric bill, the procedure is as follows: We open the C—Utilities sub-account and transfer $80.00 to C—Checking. Then we go to C—Checking and write a check to the electric company. Now to expand on the idea. Let's say that we receive $50.00 that is earmarked for the water bill. We deposit the fifty dollars into the C—Checking sub-account and then transfer it to the C—Utilities sub-account. All money coming in or going out goes through the transfer account. We reconcile with the bank just like normal, except our balance is the total of all sub-accounts within a "real" account. For example, if we are reconciling the bank statement for the checking account, the balance of the checking account is the total of all accounts that begin with a C—, and all deposits and checks from the checking account are located in the transfer account, in this case, the C—Checking account.

To do the same thing without a computer is a bit more tedious, but that is to be expected; making tedious jobs easier is one of the tremendous advantages of using a computer. Once again, I cannot stress enough that figuring a computer into your overall financial plan is more than worthwhile and need not cost an arm and a leg. Plus, contrary to the great marketing plans of the software and hardware companies, a decent computer can last for many years, and will not necessarily become obsolete as soon as the next bigger and better thing is introduced.

First, assemble as many checkbook ledgers (also known as a transaction register) as you have sub-accounts. In the case of the example that we are using, that would be four. Generally, these are free from the bank for the asking. These are the little booklets that go in the checkbook opposite the checks for writing down what checks you write, deposits, etc.

Remember, this block of instruction is but one way to perform the procedure. Understanding what we are doing with "real" accounts and sub-accounts is what matters, not the method by which it is done. Who knows, after some time getting use to it, you may decide that a divided three ring binder works best for you.

Take the first register and across the front cover in large letters (preferably with a marker) write: 1. C—Checking. Now label the remaining three in the same manner, numbering them as well as naming them. When you are through, you should have registers with the following writing on the front of them:

1. C—Checking
2. C—Utilities
3. C—Operating
4. C—Automotive

The purpose of the number is to allow you to track the registers and easily identify if one is missing and which one. With four sub-accounts, keeping track may not be too difficult, with ten or fifteen or twenty-two it begins to become tougher. Next, we take a piece of paper and list out our registers as I have done above. This master index is kept with the registers for easy referral so that if a register is missing we can always quickly identify which register it is. A brief case, office desk, or even empty check box all make suitable storage devices for the registers. But they must be stored somewhere where they will be safe and undisturbed; it is not as easy to back up a stack of registers as it is to back up the computer.

Now we follow the same basic procedure that we did on the computer:

Take the register that is labeled 1. C—Checking and enter an opening balance of $250.00. On the next transaction line, put the date, and where the check number goes, put a T for Transfer and put the payee as 2. C—Utilities and the amount as $80.00. We deduct the $80.00 from the $250.00 and show our balance as $170.00. Then we take the register labeled 2. C—Utilities. We show an opening balance as $00.00. On the next transaction line put the date. Where the check number goes, put N to indicate that this is money that was transferred in. Where it asks for the Payee, enter 1. C—Checking, since this is where the money came from. Enter the amount as $80.00. Add the $80.00 to the opening balance, in this case $00.00, and enter the new balance,

$80.00.

Returning to the main transfer ledger, C—Checking, on the next transaction line we show a transfer of $100.00 to C—Operation. In our C—Operating ledger we record the transfer in with an N and show the money coming from C—Checking. We then do the same with the $70.00 from C—Checking to C—Auto.

We are going to go through it again with illustrations now, but keep this in mind: it does not matter what you use to keep track of your sub-accounts as long as you understand the concepts and the system you use works for you. A manual system is a heck of a lot of work, but if it is what keeps you focused and it is the system that you prefer, there is nothing wrong with that. What is important is knowing where our money needs to go, where it is going, and where it has gone to!

In illustration 1 we have what the register of the transfer account, C—Checking, would look like.

C - Checking					
Date	**Number**	**Description**	**Payment**	**Deposit**	**Balance**
16 May 07	Dep	Deposit		$250.00	$250.00
16 May 07	T	C - Utilities	$80.00		$170.00
16 May 07	T	C - Operating	$100.00		$70.00
16 May 07	T	C - Auto	$70.00		$0.00
Illustration 1					

The first line dated 16 May shows that we made a deposit of $250.00. By using the letters "DEP" under the number we know that this was real money coming into the account. Real money means that the overall balance of the account is changed. Deposits raise the amount of money in the account, while Check numbers and EFT (Electronic Fund Transfers) reduce the amount of money in the account. You may come across a need for other codes for money in and out. I usually stick with these three. If I write a check, it has a check number. If money left my account without me writing a check, it is an EFT, and if money came into my account it is a DEP. If the code is a T or an N, I know that it was either transferred to another sub-account within the same physical account (T), or else it was transferred into this account from another sub-account within the same physical account (N). Transfers (N and T) do not change the balance of the physical account. It is like moving money around in our shoebox example earlier. The only thing that changes is how much money is in each can within the shoebox, or in this case, which sub-account the money is assigned to.

Returning to our illustration, the next line shows that we transferred $80.00 to C—Utilities. The ledger for C—Utilities would look similar to Illustration 2 below:

C - Utilities					
Date	**Number**	**Description**	**Payment**	**Deposit**	**Balance**
16 May 07	N	C - Checking		$80.00	$80.00
Illustration 2					

Looking at illustration 2, it is somewhat of a mirror image of the transaction that is recorded in the C—Checking ledger. The transfer (T) out of C—Checking that was logged in the Payment column is shown in the C—Utilities ledger as an In (N) and is in the Deposit column

Illustrations 3 and 4 reflect the final two transfers:

C - Operating					
Date	**Number**	**Description**	**Payment**	**Deposit**	**Balance**
16 May 07	N	C - Checking		$100.00	$100.00
Illustration 3					

C - Auto					
Date	**Number**	**Description**	**Payment**	**Deposit**	**Balance**
16 May 07	N	C - Checking		$70.00	$70.00
Illustration 4					

Now the time has come to pay that electric bill that we put the $80.00 in C—Utilities to cover. So what do we do? The first thing is in the ledger of C—Utilities we move the $80.00 back to C—Checking. Illustration 5 shows our entry in the C—Utilities ledger:

C - Utilities					
Date	**Number**	**Description**	**Payment**	**Deposit**	**Balance**
16 May 07	N	C - Checking		$80.00	$80.00
17 May 07	T	C - Checking	$80.00		$0.00
Illustration 5					

The date tells us when the transaction took place, the T in the number column tells us that it was a Transfer, which means that it left this sub-account, but it also tells us that the amount of money in the physical account has not changed.

The money went to our transfer account C—Checking. It had to go here for it to leave the physical account, because money does not enter or leave the physical account without going through the transfer account. The ledger for the C—Checking account would now look like illustration 6:

C - Checking					
Date	**Number**	**Description**	**Payment**	**Deposit**	**Balance**
16 May 07	Dep	Deposit		$250.00	$250.00
16 May 07	T	C - Utilities	$80.00		$170.00
16 May 07	T	C - Operating	$100.00		$70.00
17 May 07	N	C - Auto	$70.00		$0.00
17 May 07	101	C - Utilities		$80.00	$80.00
		Electric Company	$80.00		$0.00
Illustration 6					

The second to the last entry shows the money coming into this sub-account. The N designates this. The following line shows the money actually leaving the physical account. It left in the form of check number 101, and it went to the Electric Company.

This system looks like a lot of work. You might be wondering why go to all the bother. By having sub-accounts you can plan for your bills and even put aside the money for the bill in a manner that identifies exactly what the money is for. The benefits are too numerous to list all of them right now. But here is one example: in a regular checking account system using the numbers that we built our example on, you would show that you have $250.00. Now, you might be able to juggle around the $80.00, the $100.00 and the $70.00 for a while, but not long. What happens when the Electric bill only comes to $77.00, and the food costs $99.97? Best case is usually that the three dollars and three cents left over gets instantly designated as "extra" and blown before you even knew you had it. With our system we are going to learn to catch those instant windfalls, and to use them to our lasting advantage.

I understand that this has been a bit of a dry lesson and you might be wishing that you never hear of sub-categories ever again. But don't throw out the system just yet.

Later on in the book we will cover more advanced techniques to use with our sub-category system that will help you save money and achieve financial success. The pain will be worth it. The one thing that I can recommend to make the use of this system a lot easier is to get a computer and a financial software package!

Taxing Ourselves Into Prosperity

It has been said that government cannot tax itself into prosperity. Fortunately, we are not a government, and we can tax ourselves into a better standard of living. We will do it by using a principle that the government has been using for many decades to reduce the pain of extracting large sums of money from people. If you take a lot of money all at once from people, they will scream bloody murder. But if you take a little at a time, they won't even notice how much you are really taking. Heck, some will even claim that they are not being taxed enough! Ah, but I digress.

What we want to do is add a tax on how much we pay for things. Now there is no way that that can sound like a good thing. But in this instance it is. Let me explain, and then I will provide three real life applications that you can start using today. Imagine if sales tax doubled tomorrow. How long would you really notice? On day-to-day purchases, few people notice today. You go to the store to buy a few items, at checkout you pay more than the three items total and don't even think about it. You have been conditioned to think of sales tax as an inevitable truth. Almost a new math system: $A + B = X(A+B)$ where X is the sales tax. Well, as long as we have been programmed to think this way, let's use it to our advantage.

Our first application is the simplest. Let's say that your Checking account has $44.93. You go to the corner store and write a check for 12.33. Then you go somewhere else and spend 3.99. Now keep in mind that these are not allocated expenses. They are not coming out of a sub account, but rather straight out of the checking account. At the end of the day we are ready to update our ledger system for the days transactions. Our Checking ledger would look something like this:

C - Checking					
Date	**Number**	**Description**	**Payment**	**Deposit**	**Balance**
3 Jun 07		Beginning Balance			$44.93
4 Jun 07	444	The Corner Store	$12.33		$32.60
5 Jun 07	445	The Other Store	$3.99		$28.61
6 Jun 07		C - Self Tax	$3.61		$25.00
Illustration 7					

The first entry is simply what the balance is in the ledger. I did not want to make the diagram too complex. The second and third entries are our purchases for the day. The item of interest is the last entry. We have "taxed" ourselves whatever the amount is to make the balance of the account evenly divisible by five dollars. In this instance, I have named the ledger account to receive this additional taxing as C—Self Tax. The C at the beginning indicates that this is a sub-account contained within our physical checking account. The name Self Tax could be any name that has a meaning to you. Nor is the rounding to the next five dollars a magic number, either. Maybe times are so tough that you are not ready to pay such a large tax. If that is the case, start smaller. Do what is right for you. If nothing else, just round off the cents. Here is an example of this:

C - Checking					
Date	**Number**	**Description**	**Payment**	**Deposit**	**Balance**
3 Jun 07		Beginning Balance			$44.93
4 Jun 07	444	The Corner Store	$12.33		$32.60
5 Jun 07	445	The Other Store	$3.99		$28.61
6 Jun 07		C - Self Tax	$0.61		$28.00

Illustration 8

Now, contrary to what seems the first thing that pops into many modern individual's minds, C—Self Tax is not a "party fund". In advance we need to decide what intelligent use this money will be put to, and at what intervals. Paying down debt is a good use, as is adding to an investment that improves our financial position.

So then, let's say that we have decided to use this to fund paying off our credit card. Great. This does not mean that C—Self Tax is used for the credit card payment. It means that C—Self Tax is added to the credit card payment so that it reduces the principle beyond what we would have normally been able to achieve. That is, if we were going to pay two hundred dollars on the credit card at the end of the month, then we will pay two hundred dollars plus whatever is in the C—Self Tax file.

An easy trap to fall into must be avoided. We cannot reduce what we are going to pay on the card simply because we know that there is additional money coming from the C—Self Tax account. If we do this, we are not progressing, but simply juggling money.

If you were going to pay two hundred dollars on the account and instead pay forty dollars less because you are adding forty dollars from the C—Self Tax account, you are making no headway at all. You are fooling yourself into thinking that you are accomplishing something, and you aren't.

This brings up an interesting point—using the sub-account system only helps us if there are real world gains. Too often I see people spending enormous amount of times breaking down where their money goes and analyzing trends, without ever really improving there position. To go back to our example of the shoebox with the cans inside, no matter how you move the money from can to can, the amount of money in the box never changes. If you never pay off your debts, it doesn't matter which account the minimum payment comes from every month, you are not making progress.

OK, back on track with our self-taxation. The good thing about self taxation is you are not limited to only one tax. There are other areas where taxes can be added that will not be readily noticed but will help you in obtaining financial freedom.

The next example is the credit card tax. I love this one. This one works really well for me. I don't carry a credit card balance, so the "tax" is sort of like the interest that I'm not paying, but with a catch—it returns to me.

In my accounting system I create an account. Credit Card, for example. Since we already are using a "C" to identify the sub accounts of our checking account, we will use the letter "R" for the prefix of our credit cards. (By the way, once all credit cards are paid off, there is seldom if ever a good reason for using more than one card. I only use one credit card, so its account is simple Credit Card).

I select the letter "R" because it is the second letter in Credit Cards, since the first letter is in use. Again, whatever works for you. You may break away from my naming convention completely and use "X" for credit cards. As long as there is no ambiguity and you can keep everything straight, it is your system, use what you want.

In this example our credit card account is named "R—Credit Card. This account tracks the actual balance on the credit card. Now, in my checking account, I set up two new sub accounts. Again, names are strictly up to you. In my case, I used the following names because the credit card that I use is blue. No deep thought there. The first sub-account I named C—Bluecard. The second I named C—Bluecard Prior. All caught up? Good. Here is the operation: When I purchase something, I enter the actual amount in the Credit Card ledger. It looks like this:

R - Credit Card					
Date	**Number**	**Description**	**Payment**	**Deposit**	**Balance**
3 Jun 07		Beginning Balance			$0.00
4 Jun 07		The Corner Store	$23.99		-$23.99
5 Jun 07		Horseshoe Store	$11.99		-$35.98
Illustration 9					

The sole purpose of this ledger is to have a running accurate record of our credit card purchases. The magic will happen in our other two new sub accounts. Notice that in this sub-account we have a negative balance. This reflects that we owe the credit card company $35.98.

Now that this purchase is logged in our credit card ledger, we close the ledger. Then we open our C—Checking ledger, which is our main transfer account. We round our purchase up, and enter it like this:

C - Checking					
Date	**Number**	**Description**	**Payment**	**Deposit**	**Balance**
3 Jun 07		Beginning Balance			$100.00
4 Jun 07	T	C - Bluecard	$25.00		$75.00
5 Jun 07		C - Bluecard	$15.00		$60.00
Illustration 10					

At the end of the month, we go to our C—Bluecard ledger and perform the following action:

C - Bluecard					
Date	**Number**	**Description**	**Payment**	**Deposit**	**Balance**
3 Jun 07		Beginning Balance			$0.00
4 Jun 07	N	C - Bluecard		$25.00	$25.00
5 Jun 07	N	C - Bluecard		$15.00	$40.00
1 Jul 07	T	C - Bluecard Prior	$40.00		$0.00
Illustration 11					

What we have done is transferred the entire balance of our C—Bluecard sub-account to our C—Bluecard Prior sub-account. The C—Bluecard is reduced to zero for the new month, and the C—Bluecard Prior has all the money transferred in for the month, plus whatever funds might be there from previous months. The C—Bluecard Prior sub-account would look something like this:

C - Bluecard Prior					
Date	**Number**	**Description**	**Payment**	**Deposit**	**Balance**
30 Jun 07		Beginning Balance			$46.55
1 Jul 07	N	C - Bluecard Prior		$40.00	$86.55
Illustration 12					

When we receive the bill from the credit card company, assuming that we are not carrying a balance, we move the entire amount from C—Bluecard Prior to C—Checking, and then pay the bill from C—Checking. We reflect the payment in our R—Credit Card sub-account, reducing the balance to zero. Assuming that the entire credit card balance is our two purchases of $23.99 and $11.99 for a total balance of $35.98, here is what the transactions in the three sub-accounts would look like:

C - Bluecard Prior					
Date	**Number**	**Description**	**Payment**	**Deposit**	**Balance**
30 Jun 07		Beginning Balance			$46.55
1 Jul 07	N	C - Bluecard Prior		$40.00	$86.55
3 Jul 07	T	C - Checking	$35.98		$50.57
Illustration 13					

Illustration 13 is the money being transferred out of C—Bluecard Prior and into C—Checking.

C - Checking					
Date	**Number**	**Description**	**Payment**	**Deposit**	**Balance**
3 Jun 07		Beginning Balance			$100.00
4 Jun 07	T	C - Bluecard	$25.00		$75.00
5 Jun 07	T	C - Bluecard	$15.00		$60.00
3 Jul 07	N	C - Bluecard Prior		$35.98	$95.98
3 Jul 07	2399	R - Credit Card	$35.98		$60.00
Illustration 14					

Illustration 14 shows the money coming into C—Checking from C—Bluecard Prior and going out in the form of check number 2399 to pay off the credit card bill. The actual check goes to the credit card company, of course, but we show it in our ledger going to our R—Credit Card sub-account so we can clear our balance here.

R - Credit Card					
Date	**Number**	**Description**	**Payment**	**Deposit**	**Balance**
3 Jun 07		Beginning Balance			$0.00
4 Jun 07		Grocery Store	$23.99		-$23.99
5 Jun 07		Horseshoe Store	$11.99		-$35.98
3 Jul 07	2399	C - Checking		$35.98	$0.00

Illustration 15

You will notice that even though we charged ourselves forty dollars (fifteen dollars and twenty-five dollars) for our credit card purchases, the total amount was only really $35.98. What about the other $4.02? That is the reward—it's yours! Very similar to the self-tax in our earlier example.

You may wonder why it is necessary to have two sub accounts, C—Bluecard and C—Bluecard Prior. For you, it may not be necessary or even desired. I did it that way for a couple of reasons. First, the month ends on the last day of the month, but I don't receive the bill until a few days later. By segregating my spending this way, I knew what was available for the current month's bill. Also, by having a current sub-account and prior sub-account, it made it very easy at a glance to analyze my monthly spending.

Some might argue that I could achieve the same by looking at the R—Credit Card account. Not really. This sub-account does not reflect my five dollar round up, and this is a very real "tax" to me and is taken into account when studying my spending habits.

Two key points to make very sure that you understand from this procedure are the following:

First, remember that the balance on the R—Credit Card sub-account is a negative. Until the bill is paid, this is money that you owe.

Second, even though we show in our ledger the check for the credit card bill going to R—Credit Card, the check actually goes to the credit card company. Outside the shoebox, so to speak.

This final application of our self-taxing procedure is a very powerful one that we will call the fuel tax. How much does it cost to buy gas every time that you go to the gas station? In my case, it cost fifty bucks. Now, if you are of the SUV crowd, you may feel that that is a very good price. But I don't drive a SUV. I drive somewhat of an economy car. Then why so much, you ask? Ah, because a car does not run on gas alone! When I buy a tank of gas, I know it is more than twenty dollars but never more than twenty-five dollars, so I figure thirty dollars for gas. This covers the cost of the gas plus the five-dollar tax I charge myself for using the credit card. But I also realize that as I drive this car, it is going to need maintenance and repairs. So I figure twenty dollars for every tank of gas for this. Twenty-five plus five plus twenty. There is the fifty dollars.

Now, here is how I do it so that I don't go crazy trying to juggle the numbers. Again, in this instance computer software is highly recommended, since it allows you to have split lines on a transaction and can even "memorize" the transaction so you don't have to retype the entire transaction each time you enter it.

When I buy the fuel the first thing that I do is enter the actual amount in my R—Credit Card sub-account.

Next, there is an entry in my C—Checking sub-account called "Fuel".

Here is something like what your C—Checking sub-account would look like:

C - Checking					
Date	**Number**	**Description**	**Payment**	**Deposit**	**Balance**
4 Jul 07		Beginning Balance			$100.00
7 Jul 07	T	Fuel			$100.00
		C - Bluecard	$30.00		$70.00
		C - Auto Maintenance	$20.00		$50.00

Illustration 16

Illustration 16 reflects our fuel purchase, and breaks it down into the two sub transactions that make up this process—the $25.00 that went to C—Bluecard to pay for the gas, and the $25.00 that went into a new sub-account called C—Auto Maintenance that will help to pay for future repairs or vehicle replacement. Every time I buy gas, I know it will cost me fifty dollars. The only time this changes is when the price of gas rises substantially enough for the actual cost to exceed twenty-five dollars. At that point, fuel costs me fifty-five dollars, and I raise the amount to C—Bluecard to thirty-five dollars—thirty dollars plus five dollars. I don't adjust downward. As seldom as the price of gas significantly retreats, this is not often an issue. And since the additional money is mine anyway, why back down a price that I have grown accustomed to paying?

Where Do I Start?

First, either in a notebook or on a spreadsheet on a computer, begin a list of your monthly bills. Let's first establish where the money goes and where it needs to go.

Utilities and rent (or house payment) come to mind first. On payments with fixed amounts such as rent, it is easy to know what you pay every month. On things like utilities that are not the same amount every month, it is a little more work. If you know what you have paid over a period of time, say the last year, look at these payments and enter the largest. Not the average bill but the largest bill.

After rent and utilities, if you have a car payment, enter this. If there is more than one, enter as many as you have. Next move on to credit card bills. Again, if possible, look over the past year and enter the largest minimum payment. If you have a monthly bill for car insurance, enter this. If you pay quarterly, divide the quarterly payment by three. If you have this down to a bi-annual amount, divide by six.

After everything is entered and you look at the total month, one of three things will happen. The first is you might shrug your shoulders and say, "Yea, just what I thought". The second possibility is that you may cringe and whimper "but I don't make that much money in a month!". Or you may get excited and cheer with a resounding "I make a lot more than that!". If you respond with the third, after a short pause you might utter, "but where does the rest of it go?". Hopefully, you are either muttering the first or the third. If you are the unlucky individual that is mouthing the "but I don't make that much money in a month!" then your finances are definitely in need of life support and it is time to start separating the necessity from the luxury.

Now, as anyone that has done time in the Army can assure you, there is very little that we feel is necessary that truly is. However, we do hope to maintain some semblance of civilization, so we will accept that there are some things that we have no plans on voluntarily doing without. A place to live would be one of these. Electricity, heat, water, sewage, more pleasantries that we would rather not do without.

Next down the ladder of necessities would probably come the telephone. Not as essential as heating and sewage perhaps, but very handy to have in case of an emergency, as well as convenient in finding and maintaining employment.

As we go down the list we start facing items that may be very near and dear to our heart, but cannot be defined as critical to life with any degree of truthfulness: Cell Phone, Cable Television, Internet, Long Distance, etc. It is up to you to decide what you can or should live without. This does not mean that you have to give something up! If you can pay the bill, there is no reason to shed something you really enjoy just to be a martyr; financial success is not necessarily about living a life of hardship, but rather insuring that you never have to live a life of hardship! But. Don't you hate the "but" coming just when things are looking good? But. But the fact that you are paying for something every month does not mean that you should keep paying for it just because it is there. If you don't use it, don't need it, don't enjoy it, get rid of it and stop paying for it!

Example—a few years ago I noticed that every month my long distance bill consisted of taxes. A lot of taxes on a usage of zero. I didn't use long distance, I didn't even know anyone long distance to call. But every month I was paying money to government programs that I didn't even know about. So I called the phone company and told them that I didn't think I should be paying all of these taxes on a bill of zero. If I used the service, tax me. Otherwise, don't. The nice, polite, understanding long distance company told me tough, there was nothing I could do about it, I was paying the tax, use the service or not. I had long distance service removed from my account, effectively kicking the long distance carrier to the curb, and stopped paying all those taxes every month, while still using long distance as much as I ever did—none.

Learn to look at you bills and see what you are paying for that you don't know about and that you never use. The amount of money you can save yourself might surprise you! Now, if you are a matter of days away from being evicted and living in a residency where the property taxes alone are more than you make in a year, we might have to let that dream go. But if you are currently able to keep your head above water monthly, even if just barely and that is by robbing Peter to pay Paul, there is probably hope.

Next, now that we have somewhat of a handle on our monthly obligations, we have to identify where the rest of our money is going. Let's start with one from the headlines, fuel. If you have a concept of how much you spend on gas in a month, add it in. Otherwise, make an educated guess. And make it high. Throughout this process, it is much better to overstate your expense than to understate it.

Every little thing that you spend money on in a month must be entered. When you are finished, your list will look something like this:

Rent—$700.00
Electricity—$200.00
Heating Gas—$100.00
Groceries—$625.00
Water—$50.00
Cable—$75.00
Telephone—$90.00
Auto—$270.00

Auto Insurance—$120.00
Auto Fuel—$250.00
Entertainment—$520.00

This list brings us to a total of $3000.00. Now, you will probably have a number of other items on your list. Don't worry that it doesn't look exactly like this list.

Next, we take our list and make a sub-category in our system for each item on the list. In some cases, you may wish to combine like items into a single sub-category. For instance, Electricity, Heating Gas, Water, Cable, and Telephone might be combined into a sub-category called C—Utilities. It is very important that we track every expenditure.

Once the list is complete and we have created all the sub-categories, we create one more sub-category. You might call it something like C—Next Month (again, what you call it is up to you. For some reason when I set mine up years ago, I named it C—End Around. Whatever works for you).

Now we start saving as much money as we can and putting it into the C—Next Month. Once the C—Next Month balance is equal to the total of all of our monthly expense sub-accounts, the fun begins. At the end of the month, we transfer money from the C—Next Month to the monthly expense sub accounts as shown in illustration 17:

C - Next Month					
Date	**Number**	**Description**	**Payment**	**Deposit**	**Balance**
31 Jul 07		Beginning Balance			$3,000.00
31 Jul 07	T	Monthly			$3,000.00
		C - Rent	$700.00		$2,300.00
		C - Utilties	$515.00		$1,785.00
		C - Groceries	$625.00		$1,160.00
		C - Auto	$270.00		$890.00
		C - Auto Insurance	$120.00		$770.00
		C - Auto Fuel	$250.00		$520.00
		C - Entertainment	$520.00		$0.00
Illustration 17					

What we have now accomplished with this monumental task is a month's breathing room on all of our bills! As our bills for the following month come due, we pay them out of their own sub-account, and as we have income, we transfer it to our C—Next Month account. Once our C—Next Month account reaches the threshold of what is required for the next month's bills, in this case three thousand dollars, whatever else we make in the month we can use for other allocations, such as paying down debt, or investments.

Remember way back when we talked about using the C at the beginning of the sub-account to designate which real account it was a sub of? Well, now is the time when that becomes pertinent. Having gotten a handle on our finances, our next step up in the pursuit of financial wellness is for the money that we have sitting and waiting to be used to generate some income itself. Now, in the case of month-to-month bills, the checking account is probably OK. But what about something like the auto insurance where we are setting aside money monthly but it only goes out every six months? Or house insurance where it only leaves us annually? In these cases, we need to look for other options that will actually pay a return on this money that is just sitting there. There are a number of options available. There are bank money markets, brokerage money markets, savings accounts, as well as other accounts.

A few of the things that we need to be aware of as we begin exploring how to make our money make money for us are: What is the minimum balance? How do I deposit money? How do I withdraw money? Are there withdrawal restrictions? Is my money safe, meaning will the amount that I need be there when I need it? For the purpose we are exploring, an investment where the balance can fluctuate up and down is probably not right for this purpose.

Unexpected Expenses Will Happen. If We Know That, They Are Not "Unexpected"

A meteorite hitting the house is an unexpected expense, needing a plumber is not. Space aliens stealing your car is an unexpected expense, a flat tire is not. Growing a second head is an unexpected expense, having to have a wisdom tooth pulled is not.

Anticipate your potential expenses and set up accounts to see you through them. You might do something like an account called C—Appliances. Deposit funds into this account regularly as if it were an expense coming due. In truth, it is. When the washer, dryer, refrigerator, or some other appliance needs replacing or repairing, this fund will help defray the cost.

Given enough of a regular deposit and enough time before the repair or replacement is needed, the fund may even cover the entire expense. For these kinds of sub-accounts that may not come into play for a length of time, I try to assign them to money market accounts so that the money can work at earning some interest while awaiting its main purpose.

PART III

Bringing In The Money

About Work

After a certain point, you can only save so much. For financial success, money must come in, not just not go out. It seems that there is a point when people start pushing the envelope on how much they can save by cutting expenses. This eventually leads to a point of diminishing returns.

When this happens, you have to step back and see what is going on. An example of this happening is when you start spending great amounts of time an effort to save miniscule amounts of money. For instance, you start doing really silly, stupid things like counting the number of paperclips you use. Or worrying about how much energy the light bulb in the refrigerator is consuming. Or perhaps coming up with hair brain ideas like reusing the return envelope that comes with the utility bill. At this point, you have to recognize the energy and time you are expending and compare it to the income from the same energy and time applied to whatever it is you do to make money. Sometimes, we have to just nip the conservation fever in the bud and get up off our butts and bring in new money.

This brings up another point. Too often, I see people make a huge mistake and walk out of their employment for the most inconsequential of reasons. And they do it when they are totally unprepared to lose that weekly paycheck. I know, because I have made this mistake, it set me back probably a year or more, and would have done even greater damage if I had not had a series of lucky breaks.

Everybody gets aggravated at their job. It is a fact of life. Heck, I get aggravated at mine, and I am self-employed! The first instinct when we get our feelings hurt is to pick up our toys and go home. If we have prepared to do this, great. Unfortunately, preparedness and leaving a job in a huff seldom synchronize with each other. Worse, once we walk out, several things often become apparent. The insult might not have been as serious as we first deemed it to be. Or perhaps our expectation of what we are worth is not recognized as readily by others.

A great misunderstanding is the fact that even though we are being paid X by a particular company, there may be few or no other companies willing to pay us anything like that amount. Like many things in life, when we most need a job is when there are none, and when we are not looking for a job, there are great opportunities around every corner.

When preparing to leave a job, one of the first things you will need to know is how much money you will need to make to equal what you make with the job now. If you live paycheck to paycheck, and make six hundred dollars a week, you will need at least six hundred dollars a week.

Here is a common pitfall. Many people will say that they only take home four hundred and forty dollars a week due to taxes, so if they make four hundred and forty dollars a week, they will be OK. Take it from a guy that made this error in judgment, it is no fun to take out a huge cash advance on your credit card the next April to pay the income taxes. The taxman doesn't care about a whole lot beyond getting his money, and if you quit your job and need the tax money to pay your bills, he will be quite unsympathetic, to say the least!

Establish What Is Financial Success

You have to decide what you want out of life. Be exact and concrete. This does not mean that you cannot change and modify this goal as time goes by, but it gives you a target to shoot for and a way to gauge your progress, and to know when you arrive at success. You cannot simply say, “I want to be rich”. Believe it or not, as you become more successful, your concept of rich will change substantially. I can remember times in my life where I said that if I could make six bucks an hour, I would be set for life, and I can remember looking on eight dollars an hour as a wage scale reserved for people with far more training and education than I could ever have. I have felt that if I could make $24,000 dollars a year I would be very comfortable, and I have felt the same thing about $100,000 a year. You have to establish what you want out of life, and what it will cost.

There is an old saying that says, “Money can’t buy happiness”. Whenever I hear that I feel that it must have started out as the mantra of a quitter that wanted an excuse. Change the context around a bit and play with the quote and the stupidity becomes a bit clearer. “Money can’t buy health”. No, but it can buy food to keep you from starving and medicine when you are sick. “Money can’t change the weather”. Again, no it can’t. But it can take you to a climate more to your liking. And how about the classic “money can’t buy you love”. It can buy you the freedom to spend more time looking for love, as well as make you more attractive to the opposite sex. I don’t mean in physical appearance, but rather what you have to offer the relationship.

This may sound shallow at first, but think about it. Nobody gives the homeless guy on the corner a good long look in case he is their soul mate and just a bit down on his luck right now. Go on a date and share with your companion that you are facing pending bankruptcy, loss of job and possible homelessness. Ask to borrow some money, and stress that you might not be able to pay it back, and you need it in a quantity much larger than he or she carries with them. The chances of a second date have just gone way down. And I wouldn’t count on the sizable loan, either.

I am not preaching that materialism is everything. You can be filthy rich and totally miserable. All you have to do is set your mind to it. But if you set your mind to being happy, money can help you to find this happiness and contentment in your life.

Life is Dynamic, Not Static

What is the right choice, the right investment, the right purchase today is not the right answer tomorrow. Everything in life is constantly shifting and changing, so your Master Plan must be able to be changed as well. In investments, today's darlings are tomorrow's dogs. What is a prudent selection today can be fool hearty tomorrow. You have to continuously be alert to the world around you and to your own personal circumstances to insure that your Master Plan stays on track. Here is a project to understand the fluidity of life. Get on the freeway and drive twenty or so miles while there is a fair amount of traffic. You will notice that the best lane to be in does not always remain the best lane. If up ahead there is an accident in that lane, this best lane will probably become the worst lane very quickly.

Watch the other drivers. Notice how many of them are very oblivious to anything happening more than one car in front of them. Many of them will not even look far enough ahead to see their exit fast approaching until the last minute. For some, the exit will even be missed due to their inattention. Worse, the inattentive driver may even do some very unsafe freeway acrobatics of jumping two or three lanes and cutting off other drivers just to make their exit. Most amazing of all? These people will swear with total sincerity that they are excellent drivers since they have not had an accident, even though their accident free record is in spite of their driving skills and because of the driving skills of others.

This is how many people approach life and personal finance. They don't look to the future, they don't plan, and they make the most hazardous of spur of the moment decisions when faced with the unexpected, even though it could have been totally anticipated and planned for if they had simply looked a little further ahead. And how do these people rationalize their financial life and equate it to being "good drivers"? They use the yardstick that they have managed to pay the minimum payment on their bills and that nobody is suing them this month.

Of course, some people have very flexible yardsticks, and even these two items are not always true. For some people, the fact that they have a place to sleep tonight and the repo man hasn't come for the car yet is viewed as a winning situation. This is the equivalent of freeway acrobatics, and the more you do it the sooner the big crash happens.

PART IV

Putting The Money To Work

Investment and Strategies

Now we have entered the advanced section of the book. I will address some of the investment vehicles that I am acquainted with on a first hand bases. You will find no recommendations here. As I have seen through the years, today's dogs are tomorrow's darlings. I will however share with you some of the realities of the particular investment as I have experienced it.

One of the things that I will do for you is to encourage you to consider what your investment goals are. Often the biggest thing in an investors mind is how soon can they sell the investment for a profit. Is this the best thing?

Stocks

When it comes to common stocks, the theories abound on just what makes the right choice. And to complicate matters, times are always changing, and what is right today might not be right tomorrow. Nothing exemplifies this as much as a story that I recall from my days selling mutual funds. To display the relative safety of the blue chip fund, I would outline the companies that made up this fund, and I would stress how the big player in the list would have to hit rocky times. I would ask the client if they could even imagine that happening. Well, now years later, I have seen that exact scenario come to pass as those untouchable companies have fallen on hard times indeed.

When I look at a stock, I take in a number of different things. Is it a one trick pony, or is there some diversity within the company? Is it of a large enough size and trading at a high enough price that I am comfortable with it fitting into the guidelines that I have set? Does it pay dividends, and what is the yield? What is the price to earnings ratio? There are a number of things that I look at when considering a common stock.

You will notice one that is not listed that is usually on everybody's mind, and that is what is the potential for an increase in the price per share. I don't care. I am not looking for a quick one-time profit. I am more interested in long and steady and fitting into my master plan.

Mutual Funds Load VS No Load

Load versus no load is always an interesting question. Understand, all a load is is a sales charge on a mutual fund. You may pay it when you buy the fund, you may pay it when you sell the fund. If it is a no load fund, you don't pay that particular charge. I don't like paying any more money than I have to. But what someone else makes when I invest is not something that I spend a lot of time thinking about. I am more concerned with what I am going to make.

If one mutual fund is paying historically five percent over the past three years with no load, and a comparable fund is paying fifteen percent for the same period but has a five percent front load, all else being equal, I am paying a load.

It is amazing to listen to people talk and to realize that quite often people are less interested in their own profits than they are in what the salesman is making on the deal. To hear these folks talk, they would rather lose money than pay a load and turn a profit! If you are getting a deal that you consider a good deal, let the other guy make some money, too. Worry about your bottom line, not someone else's.

Money In The Bank

Money in the bank is good for a number of things. As a stash awaiting opportunity, or perhaps something set aside for a rainy day. Not for long term growth.

Time deposits such as certificates of deposits can make a fine addition for an investment portfolio, and I have seen times when the yield was very impressive, indeed. But I don't think money in the bank should make up an entire investment portfolio. There are too many opportunities out there to settle on one bland option.

Collectibles

The collectible market can be a fun hobby, and in some cases even an effective investment tool. But don't forget, there has to be a buyer for your collectible to have any value, and history is full of collectibles that went from being worth a king's ransom one day to being of sentimental value at best a short time later. And as I pointed out before, there is no government agency in charge of what something is worth.

If you invest in something and then find there are no buyer when you are ready to sell, it is best if it is something that you can enjoy for its own merits. If you love comics and want to invest in comics, great, but if you can't stand the things and invest in them solely for the perceived future value, you may someday find a stack of worthless books on your hands that you cannot even enjoy reading.

Real Estate Flipping

Real estate flipping has been the big get rich quick thing in recent years. Flipping is the slang term for buying a house, fixing it up, and reselling it. When I hear about flipping, I have to wonder what people are thinking! In my opinion, this one form of investing has almost every pitfall known to man! It is labor intensive, either your labor or a hired worker, is often predicated upon completion of the renovation and reselling of the property within a certain amount of time, and is just dependent on too many unknowns. The house has to be bought, fixed up—both the repairs that you knew about when you bought the property as well as the ones that you discovered after you were an owner, a buyer must be found—not just someone that wants to buy the house, but someone who actually has the money and/or credit to do so, and the closing must occur as soon as possible so that the number of monthly payments can be kept to a minimum, as well as utilities and accumulating property taxes. And the market must remain agreeable while you are waiting for the close. What if something happens in the economy and lenders dry up? You may get to keep the house for a long, long time. I get flustered just writing about it. No thank you!

Real Estate Rental Truths

There are definite realities associated with investing in real estate rental properties, and for some reason, I rarely see these truths mentioned on infomercials.

I started investing in real estate rental properties in the early eighties, and these truths are every bit as real today as they were twenty years ago. The infomercials always make it seem that finding a lender and purchasing the property delivers you to the Promised Land. In my experiences, this is where the troubles start, not end.

If you are going to be renting the property, all you have to do is get the tenants in, collect the rent, use the rent to make the payment, and pocket the difference. Or so the story goes.

For me, it has seldom worked that way. The story usually goes more likc this: Thc housc needs a number of repairs before it can be rented, so spend some money. The house is empty so pay the mortgage. Tenants are found, but can't move in until mid-month. Only collected one half month's rent, so pay the mortgage again with the shortage coming out of my pocket. Tenants are late on next month's rent, so pay mortgage again out my own pocket and hope I can collect the past due rent and recover some of my money.

Property taxes go up, and now the rent doesn't even cover the monthly mortgage. Welcome to the world of negative cash flow. Every month, in addition to collecting rent, I have to put some of my money with it to pay the mortgage. Repairs are needed, more expense. And so it goes.

Am I saying real estate is a bad investment? Not at all. At the time of this writing, my wife and I own three rental properties. What I am saying is that you need to understand the way the business really is. You need money. It is called cash flow for a reason. It flows, and often only in one direction for stretches of time. And counting on uncollected rent from currently non-existent renters is not the soundest of gambles.

Real estate provides some good tax advantages, as well as a pretty good chance of turning a profit through property appreciation. And when the plan really comes together and the tenants are in the house and paying their rent on time, and there are no pending repairs and the cash flow is positive, everything can really look rosy. Don't get too used to it, it probably won't last.

Making money is work, and making money in real estate is no exception. One piece of advice I would offer is to spend a little money and use a real estate management company. I don't believe the hassle of even one late night phone call about a plumbing problem is worth saving the money that a professional management company charges. Besides, it frees you up to pursue other way of achieving your dreams.

Paid Financial Advisors

In my opinion, and my experience, not worth it. Between regulatory requirements and in house regulations, it seems that the advice is often timid and even ambiguously meaningless. A story comes to mind from the early eighties when I asked my broker at the time about a particular floundering company. His sage wisdom was something to the effect that if the company recovered I could make some money, but if they went bankrupt, I could lose some money. How profound is that? Just to finish the story, I did buy into the company, they did recover, and I used the profits to fund the down payment on my first income property. Needless to say, the advice had no bearing on my decision.

Where To Start

So how do you learn enough about these and other different investment opportunities to make an educated decision and get started? Well, obviously, I am not providing you with enough information to do that. And with good reason. First, as I have pointed out numerous times throughout this book, the world is constantly changing.

What I might consider today to be the greatest investment ever available may be nothing but a money pit by the time that you read this. Also, any investment should be selected with an overall consideration of your Master Plan in mind. And, since your Master Plan is going to be different from my Master Plan, what is right for me is not necessarily what is right for you. Let's face it. People are different, also. People make money in real estate, people make money in stocks, people make money in mutual funds, and people make money in gold and a thousand other investments. Other people lose money in all of these things. You have to invest intelligently in what is right for you, at the right time. You research. You read, you pay attention to the world around you, and you ask questions. You are the one looking at investing the money, put forth the time and effort to learn about what you are looking at. Get the facts, and get various opinions, and learn to tell the difference. Remember, facts are not concrete. What is true today may not be true tomorrow, so always check the timeliness of your research material.

PART V

Putting It All Together

Now is the point where we put the entire book together into a usable plan. First, we have to make the decision that we want to succeed. If you are happy living pay check to paycheck and do not really desire a better life, there is no need to go any further. But if you are willing to put forth the effort, then you are in prime starting position.

Once you determine that you want a better life, you must identify what this means and devise a plan to get there. What is a better life? Is a better life an extra beer on Friday night, or is a better life one in which you are free to travel at will instead of working forty plus hours a week on someone else's schedule. After "A Better Life" is defined, you must put together a plan of action on how to get there. Among other things, this plan of action must contain concrete numbers of what finances will be required to achieve the goal.

Determining all this, you must now determine if "A Better Life" is worth getting the monkey off your back, if there is one. I did it, and you can, too. You might feel that I didn't give enough information on how to beat addiction. If you think this way, you are deluding yourself. I told you everything you need to know. Plain and simple, just do it. Addiction is a life choice. Save the "illness" story for enablers. It won't work on me.

I remember once when I got thrown in jail due to alcohol and needed my parents to bail me out. I was dreadfully worried about facing my mother. I was ashamed, and didn't know what I was going to say. When I finally saw her, she started telling me about how it wasn't my fault, my biological father had been a heavy drinker and it was in my genes. I could not believe my good fortune! While I nodded my head in my most serious expression, in my mind I was thinking that this was truly a load of crap, but if she believed it, I would go along with it.

I've been an addict, don't give me the bleeding heart stories. I have been addicted to alcohol, I have been addicted to tobacco, and I have done drugs. I overcame all of them. This doesn't mean that I deserve a medal, it simply means that I know first hand that you can shake the monkey off if that is what you want. If you instead choose to believe how it is an illness and how you are powerless, you are hiding from the truth. And the truth is, you can get clean and stay clean if you want to. Nobody can overcome your addiction for you. You must want to do it, and only you can do it.

I will offer this further bit of advice, though. You will find that you have a huge amount of spare time on your hands, which has a great tendency to lead right back to using. A great number of winners fill this spare time with religious devotion. Also, many others use the time to pursue higher education. The colleges are full of recovering addicts. Successfully recovering addicts. I have run into many people that have traded the monkey for one heck of a lot of life improving education! Find what interests you, and pursue it!

Realize and accept that shaking the monkey off is the only way to find long-term success.

I know about the wonderful master plans that will come to an addict that appear to offer a way to succeed and keep the addiction both. They won't work.

I remember one of my own twisted schemes that at the time seemed like the answer to everything. I reasoned that with the strength of my love for beer, which was in truth an addiction to alcohol, I would always find a way to buy beer. As long as I saved the cans from all the beer, I would eventually be rich. The more I drank, the richer I would be! Yep, to my pickled brain, this was indisputable logic!

Forget the plans that let you stay addicted, they are as delusional as is believing that it is an illness that you cannot overcome.

Next, you must insure that the people in your life have the same goal as you. You cannot win a financial battle when someone else is racking up the bills faster than you can make the money.

Get you mind straight about money, and what is necessary for your master plan to become a reality. There is only one type of money, real money. There is not extra money, found money, change money, or any of the other names that encourage waste. There is only money.

Determine to cut the money you pay on money to a minimum. Get out of debt and lower your interest rates at every opportunity. Always look to better your position.

Once your position is in good shape as far as what you are paying, start looking at your money and insure that it is working to bring in other money and not just sleeping on the job. Money that is waiting to pay a bill in full, such as insurance, so that no interest is paid is a good thing. Money that is earning interest while it does this is an even better thing.

Identify waste, and recognize when you are buying something because of image as opposed to buying something because it suits your needs. Image is nice, but wait to buy it until after you arrive on Success Street, or you may never get there.

Find a system to track your money and your bills and obligations and make the most of it. You can use my system, develop you own, a combination of the two, or someone else's. The origin of the system is not important as long as it works. Whatever the system, make sure that it is real. On paper or on a computer. None of this nonsense of having it all in you head. That is not a system, that is you lying to yourself again.

Remember that once expenses are cut to a reasonable minimum, bringing in more money is where it is at. Don't waste huge sums of time trying to squeeze one more nickel of savings, put the work into bringing in more dollars. It is a balancing act, and dollars earned have more weight than nickels saved.

With expenses slashed and work maximized, look for ways to invest your money for even more returns. Remember there is no magic investment, if it is too good to be true it probably isn't true, and that yesterday's dogs can be today's darlings, and what is the smart money today may be the money pit tomorrow. Never forget that smart investing is work. If it wasn't, everybody would be rich.

Never stop. Fight complacency and always look to improve your position. There will be plenty of time to be content with where you are after they lower you into the ground. Strive for improvement, that is the heart of the human condition.

Afterward

Oct 9, 2017

And there you have it, the first book in the Looking Past the Next Paycheck series. The original publishing of the book did not have this afterward. At the time, I didn't know that Looking Past the Next Paycheck was going to be the first in a series of books just like right now I don't know if there will be more than two.

Yes, that is a roundabout way to announce that the sequel to this book will soon be available. It will be entitled Ten Thousand Soap Boxes - Looking Past the Next Paycheck Book II.

A number of things contributed to the decision to write a second book. First, there were a lot of positive comments about this book from people who have read it, and I have had multiple requests from those readers for another book.

Also, time has moved on, presenting me with more material. This book is the length it is because I neither wanted to repeat myself or to beat on a comment well beyond the point where I should have quit.

In my mind, I had always said that if there were to be another book, it would have to be new material. I never wanted to just recycle the same stories that I have already told, and in the next volume, I do believe that I have succeeded in providing fresh concepts without rehashing what the readers of this book have already read.

Even though the material for the second book has been in the works for some time now, I have no idea if and when I would have ever completed it on my own. A large part of the credit for the re-release of this book as well as the completion and release of the next book must go to my new production editor Mr. Eric Daugherty. Without Mr. Daugherty's efforts, limbo may have indeed been a permanent state for my future writings.

Finally, for those who have glimpsed the early drafts of the Orion Banks fiction series, and particularly those who have encouraged me to finish at least the first book and get it published, it looks like it will finally happen.

The first book in the Orion Banks series is scheduled to be the next book written after the release of Ten Thousand Soap Boxes - Looking Past the Next Paycheck Book II.

Robert L. Robinson

Made in the USA
Monee, IL
04 November 2026

67387889R00067